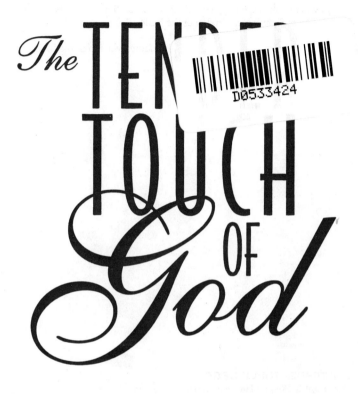

The TENDER TOUCH OF God

MIKE MACINTOSH

HARVEST HOUSE PUBLISHERS
Eugene, Oregon 97402

Except where otherwise indicated, Scripture quotations in this book are taken from the New King James Version of the Bible.

Verses marked KJV are taken from the King James Version of the Bible.

THE TENDER TOUCH OF GOD
Copyright © 1996 by Harvest House Publishers
Eugene, Oregon 97402

MacIntosh, Mike, 1944–
    The tender touch of God / Mike MacIntosh.
        p. cm.
    ISBN 1-56507-408-4 (alk. paper)
    1. Christian life. 2. Spiritual healing.   I. Title.
    BV4501.2.M237   1996
    248.8'6—dc20   95-42617
                               CIP

Printed in the United States of America.

96 97 98 99 00 01 02 / BC / 10 9 8 7 6 5 4 3 2 1

Contents

Part One:
Stop the Bleeding

Part Two:
Dress the Wound

Part Three:
Let God Heal

Dedicated to Dr. Sherwood Eliot Wirt,
Editor Emeritus, Decision Magazine,
who has prodded me for years to
begin a writing career. He has been a
mentor, a father, a brother, a counselor,
an advisor, a saint and a friend to me.
When I grow up I want to be just like Woody.

Foreword

Years ago a friend in England asked me to write a foreword to a book a publisher had asked her to write. She had been struck by some crippling disease that left her confined to a wheelchair. She—a lovely young mother with a husband and six children. And she was nearly driven crazy by Christians who kept saying, "There must be some unconfessed sin in your life, otherwise God would heal you." So, she wrote an excellent little book called *Beyond Healing*. It had a real ministry, pointing readers back to the comforting arms of our loving God.

The Tender Touch of God by Mike MacIntosh reminds me of that superb little book. It, too, helps people deal with their pains and hurts by pointing them back to our loving Savior. I believe Mike is well qualified to write such a book; Bill and I have known and loved him for years. He knows the hurts of people, and he is eager to help them discover God's unfailing love in the midst of their hurts.

After the Oklahoma City disaster, Bill was asked to go and comfort those devastated by grief. He, our son Franklin, and I visited the bomb site and were being driven in three little golf carts right up to the front of the demolished building. Bodies were still buried beneath the wreckage; men were busy cleaning away trash. One man, pushing a heavy broom and wearing dusty worker's garb, looked up as we arrived. It was Mike. We had time only for a quick hug, then we three Grahams were off again. Later we found out that Mike was feeling rotten, but with that big smile on his face, no one would have guessed it. Our brief encounter remained the one bright spot in an otherwise dark day (you can read more about Mike's encounters in Oklahoma City later in this book).

For me, physical sufferings are minor because of good doctors and pain control. It is when I have been going through spiritual trials that the Bible becomes clearer and the most relevant to me, and the presence of the Lord Jesus all but visible. In 1974 I fell out of a tree while building a pipe slide for the grandchildren, and awoke a week later in the hospital with numerous broken bones and a concussion. My memory was gone and I remember praying, "Lord, take anything You want—but please give me back my Bible verses!" Instantly there flashed in my mind: "I have loved thee with an everlasting love, therefore with lovingkindness have I drawn thee." I had no recollection of memorizing that verse and did not know where it was in the Bible, but it was just what I needed. Bit by bit the rest returned, and after tests, the Mayo Clinic reassured me my memory loss was only temporary.

I cannot say enough about the importance of memorizing Scripture. Not just verses, but whole passages, like Romans 3:31-39; John 1:1-5, 9-14; Psalm 19:7-11. (I list these as they are the ones I have most recently memorized. The older you get, the longer it takes, but you *can* do it!) No one can take away the verses you have committed to memory. When you can't sleep, they are there; when you are in pain, they are there; when you are driving, they are there. And once they are there, they are there *anytime!* There is nothing in the whole world that speaks to one's heart like the Bible—even a verse, or a part of a verse.

Mike understands this principle well, and that's why he has peppered his book with the wisdom of God as it is found in the Bible. There is nothing in the world that speaks to one's heart like the Bible—especially in the

midst of some terrible hurt. How good it is to be reminded that God does care, that He does love us, and
that He will act on our behalf. As Mike says, there is
nothing like God's tender touch.

—*Ruth Bell Graham*

Introduction

Today, millions of people are living lonely, depressed lives, full of anxiety, pain, suffering, and hurts. In great desperation they are searching for the meaning of life and the answers to its agonizing problems.

One only has to turn on the television set and watch the talk shows of Montel Williams, Sally Jesse Raphael, Oprah Winfrey, Geraldo, or Ricki Lake to see that many people are not living their lives to the fullest. Instead, they are trapped by life's issues which have wrecked their homes and debilitated their relationships with others. The stories of many of these talk-show guests are sad and pathetic, rife with perversion, hate, racism, or some other sick condition. Others are entangled in family dilemmas that twist and warp their very personalities.

Unfortunately, 30 to 60 minutes (interrupted by a dozen commercials) never allows time for healing to take place. At the end of the show the participants and audience are left unfulfilled—feeling almost as if they've been to a circus sideshow.

Many Kinds of Hurts

Although these shows focus almost exclusively on bizarre or perverse kinds of pain, we all know that hurt wears many faces.

The death of a loved one has to be the ultimate hurt, especially when that death comes unexpectedly and in the prime of life. When my own brother was killed in a car accident many years ago, the overwhelming pain nearly swept me away with its tidal force. Yet there is healing for such pain. Physical pain is another area that's often so excruciating for us to deal with. For the past four years I have suffered a lot of discomfort from my back. I found myself tired all of the time and not sleeping well. When I went to the Mayo Clinic for a full checkup, nothing was found that could explain these symptoms. Then I noticed that I had been taking a lot of Excedrin. I quit taking it, and a few weeks later realized that I had been masking the constant discomfort in my back. Now I know the source of this pain and am on a regular fitness regimen and seeing a physical therapist to correct the problems.

The point? We can mask pain with medication, but that never gets rid of it. In fact, in most cases, over a long period of time, it only increases the agony. But when we face these hurts and take action to address them, physical hurts can often be rehabilitated and strength can return to the injured area.

The same thing is true with emotional hurts. Emotional hurts come in so many varieties. It is extremely tempting to try to mask them rather than deal with them. These inner hurts get masked so quickly and cleverly that sometimes it takes months or even years to discover the real source of our problem. Yet as long as we cover up these hurts and refuse to deal with their source, we will inevitably lose the joy of living.

My friend Hal Kuykendahl told me of his days in Vietnam. Hal is a much-decorated veteran of the Navy SEALS. Because he's seen a lot of combat, countless "war stories" are locked up in his mind. Yet he can freely talk of horrific experiences that would make a blockbuster movie. He can express what he saw and experienced—both the reality and the ugliness of it—with great sensitivity. He is a humble, gentle man—a great father, husband, and friend. Fortunately, Hal is able to keep his past in perspective and so live a very fruitful life. We'll talk more about how he is able to do this later in this book.

On the other hand, I have visited with other veterans over the years who have been unable to forget their horrifying memories of battle. They find themselves trapped in bitterness, anger, or hardness of heart. Some swing to the opposite end of the spectrum and are filled with fear, paranoia, or anxiety. They have been stripped of emotional strength and are unable to cope with everyday life.

I remember one of the first counseling appointments I had as a young minister. An engaged couple had come to me for premarital counseling. It was 1973 and the Vietnam War still was making front-page headlines. When the young man came into the office with his bride-to-be, he was wearing an army fatigue jacket. Somehow the conversation turned to the war, and he explained he had just been discharged. Though he was outgoing and talkative, I sensed a problem.

After 30 minutes of listening, he began pouring out story after story of the ugly things he had seen in jungle fighting. He was burdened by deep mental hurts and, unbeknownst to him, he was emptying out his anguish and pain.

Eventually, I turned to the young lady and asked if she realized the depth of pain in this man's heart. She said he never talked to her about the war and usually changed the subject as soon as it came up. I then asked him if he knew he was reliving these episodes in front of us. He didn't have the slightest intention of discussing this subject matter, but he said it sure felt good to unload.

Mental pains and hurts are just as real as the pain caused by getting hit on the head with a stray golf ball—and they can be just as dangerous if not attended to. We can be scarred for life if we do not deal with the things that bother us the most. Just as I covered up my back pain for a long time with medication, so emotional hurts can be easily and cleverly masked. How many times do people ask us, "How are you doing?" and we respond, "Oh, just great!"—when in reality we are suffering through one of the worst days of our life.

Going in Circles

A schoolteacher went into a department store to purchase some items for her seventh-grade class. She asked the clerk if he had any compasses in stock. "We have," he answered, "compasses for making circles, but not for going places."

Oftentimes we confuse the two. We go on our way, masking our pain, satisfied with just making circles. Sometimes those circles get bigger and bigger, but they're circles nonetheless. What a waste! Our lives are much too valuable for that. We need to be going places. Let's not settle for wandering around in endless loops.

In recent years doctors have discovered a virus that zaps people of strength and energy, preventing them from functioning at normal capacities. The virus causes what is known as "the Epstein-Barr Syndrome." The media has tagged the sickness with the title "yuppie disease," since the condition is found predominantly among the baby boom generation.

After much research with thousands of sufferers, we now know this is a real disease, inflicted by a real virus that can be identified through a blood test. This disease often comes between husbands and wives. The healthy partner just can't understand why his or her once-energetic spouse is now as inert as a ball of fluff flopping around in the clothes dryer.

Over the past several years I have noticed in counseling that personal struggles, pain, and hurts can seem to produce symptoms remarkably similar to the Epstein-Barr

Syndrome. It's as if our pain causes us to use the wrong kind of compass: We go in circles but never end up anywhere. Our pain drains us of energy; it takes all our strength just to get out of bed and try to act as if we are participating in our everyday activities.

Yet we don't have to spend the rest of our lives in this dreary state of existence. Mere existence is not *living*. Jesus said, "I have come that they may have life, and that they may have it more abundantly" (John 10:10). It is possible to break the circle of mental exhaustion. To break the circle of misery. To break the circle of hurt and pain that life has dealt to us. It is possible to live a vibrant life, full of great satisfaction and deep joy. If we invite God into our life during these dark times, we can see our struggles miraculously turning into victories.

Problems Are Only Opportunities

All human beings must face two experiences: life and death. These are the common denominators between all of us. Life and death are the bookends, and everything we experience in between makes up the volumes we call "My Life."

We have little control over many aspects of our life and death. The hurt, pain, and suffering that we encounter in life will either destroy a person or make him more productive. In some sad cases, they actually drive people to end their lives. Yet I believe that the late Corrie ten Boom was correct when she used to say, "Problems are only opportunities."

These uncomfortable experiences of life often do not allow us to control them when they enter our lives, but in most cases we can exercise both damage control and learning control. How can you and I overcome the great obstacles that confront us? How can we learn from the painful situations that we sometimes inflict unknowingly upon ourselves? Is it even possible?

You may think it's much like the story about a mother asking her son about proverbs. She asked, "Cleanliness is next to . . . what?" After a pause, the little boy answered, *"Impossible!"*

Has your emotional pain programmed you to believe that it is next to impossible for you to find relief? Then read on, my friend—this book is for you. I want to bring you hope. Hope so great, so wonderful, that you will discover the glorious joy of living. Let's begin a journey and discover together—through the lives of real people—how we can not only cope with the pains of life, but also triumph in them.

God's Healing Regimen

Many years ago as a young soldier going through basic training at Fort Ord, California, I was taught how to save a life on the battlefield. It was a simple memory lesson:

Stop the Bleeding
Start the Breathing
Dress the Wound

God, in His great wisdom, has also provided a basic pattern for dealing with our hurts. God's plan resembles that of the United States Army:

Stop the Bleeding
Dress the Wound
Let God Heal

As we've just noted, hurts come to people in many forms. Often, while "bleeding" does not take the form of red blood, the hemorrhaging is just as real. So does God's healing regimen work when the hurt is emotional? Or how about drug-induced? The answer is "Yes!" God prescribes the same basic treatment: Stop the bleeding, dress the wound, and let God heal. He, and He alone, is the Healer. And what a job He does!

The Tender Touch of God is organized according to this divine healing regimen.

In the first part, "Stop the Bleeding," we'll look more closely at what untreated pain does to us and how some of us try unsuccessfully to deal with it. We'll take whole chapters to consider four special cases of pain: the death of a loved one, serious accidents, family issues, and the refusal to deal with old hurts.

In Part Two, "Dress the Wound," we'll discuss our part in the healing process. What does God ask us to do? What steps must we take to get beyond the pain and hurt and take hold once more of the abundant life?

The third and final part of the book is no doubt the most important. "Let God Heal" focuses on the crucial and indispensable role God must play in our lives if we wish to find the joy and excitement that He intends for us.

Like you, I've had my share of hurts. During my life, I either refused to deal with those hurts, didn't know how to deal with them, or didn't know I even had them. The road back to joy has not always been easy, but it has been more than worth it. God does heal!

Hurts Are Not Your Life

Hurts, pains, sufferings. They are not your life. You cannot allow circumstances to drain the life out of you.

The psalmist cried out, "Why are you cast down, O my soul? And why are you disquieted within me? Hope in God, for I shall yet praise Him for the help of His countenance" (Psalm 42:5).

Last week my wife said to me as I was complaining again about the pain in my back, "Maybe once you write this book, you'll be healed. You are feeling what the reader is feeling." Well, if that's the case, let's get on with the book!

Before we continue, though, let me encourage you that there is hope for you. You can feel better. It will not always be easy—working against pain seldom is, whether the pain is physical or emotional. But there is hope. It is going to take courage, but you can do it! You don't have to pay an enormous price—just a small amount of your faith.

Because I am of Scottish descent, I have always enjoyed traveling throughout Scotland. The people have such a great sense of humor. They love to tell stories about their stinginess and miserly ways.

One such story concerns two Scotsmen who were traveling in the Holy Land. When they came to the Sea of Galilee and discovered that it would cost them 50 dollars each to cross the lake by boat, they protested vehemently. "The lakes of Scotland are the most beautiful lakes in the world, and one can cross them for a few shillings," one of them fumed. His guide replied, "Oh, but this is the lake Jesus walked on!" The Scotsman quickly retorted, "Small wonder, at the prices you charge for taking a boat!"

Remember, God wants to give you His tender touch. There is no price to receive it, because the price already has been paid on the cross for you. As Jesus Christ hung dying on Calvary, He cried out with His last breath, "It is finished."

I hope this book will allow you to embrace the miracle of God healing your hurts. We need not make up excuses explaining why the hurt still plagues us. We don't need to have all the answers to our hurts. Just a small bit of faith—let's say, the size of a mustard seed—and God can work a miracle in our lives. Let's give Him that chance to heal our hurts.

PART ONE
Stop the Bleeding

The Tender Touch of God

1

Pain-Distorted Personalities

—*The Tender Touch of God*—

Have you ever been to a state fair or carnival? Amusement parks usually have a fun zone. Remember the funny mirrors that could make you look ten feet tall and skinny as a bean pole? How about the ones that made you look four feet tall or as fat as a cow? We know these mirrors don't do the normal job of a mirror, which is to reflect normally what is in front of them. We laugh at the images in these mirrors because they are distorted. They give a warped image of reality. We know we aren't ten feet tall and skinny as a bean pole. The warped perspective comes from a distortion of reality.

Something like that can happen to us when we are gravely hurt; we distort the reality of the pain. It's like when we break a bone. Our body naturally goes into shock to protect us from the reality of what just took place.

The Shock of Injury

Some time ago my wife, Sandy, missed a couple of steps on our staircase, fell, and broke her leg. It was nasty. The leg bone punctured her skin, requiring a specialist to surgically repair it. Once it was repaired, a rod with screws was attached to the outside of her leg, while set screws were placed inside her leg. She was alone when the accident occurred, and before the paramedics got to our house, she had gone into shock.

Fortunately, our daughter Megan came home from high school only minutes after the accident. Sandy called to her from the second floor and told her not to come upstairs but to call 911 and get help immediately. I received a call at the office and hurried home. When I arrived, the ambulance carrying Sandy was already pulling away from the house. I stopped the paramedics and asked if I could see her and pray for her before she went to the hospital. It was obvious when I saw her that she was in shock. She was awake and coherent, but definitely in shock.

It is possible that the trauma you face has done something similar to you. You're in shock, your feelings are "numbed out." Yes, you are awake. Yes, it has been weeks, months, or even years since the incident. Nevertheless, the image you perceive of life is distorted. Most of the time you know this only on the subconscious level, but every once in a while the realization rises to the surface. *Is this how things really are?* you wonder. *Are things ever going to get better?*

If you don't deal with your hurt immediately, it can warp your personality. You're bleeding, and you must take immediate action to stop the bleeding. Otherwise, the pain can warp your personality.

I'll Get You!

Some people respond to their hurt by seeking revenge. It is said that Abe Lemmons was asked if he was bitter at University of Texas athletic director Deloss Dodds, who fired Lemmons as the Longhorn's basketball coach. "Not at all," he replied. "But I plan to buy a glass-bottomed car so I can watch the look on his face when I run over him."[1] While I am sure this was said in jest, revenge is a committed lifestyle for many people who have been hurt.

One of Bruce Willis' smash-hit movies was titled: *Die Hard (with a Vengeance)*. Hollywood has filled theaters around the world with movies featuring revenge in a starring role. Take your pick. *The Revenge of*:

- Killer Tomatoes
- Batman
- Zorro
- Etc., etc. (you fill in the blanks)

We've all heard the phrase, "Don't get mad, get even." I heard a story the other day that illustrates the idea. There was a widow who expected to receive all her deceased husband's wealth. She gave him a nice funeral and an expensive headstone, only to discover when the will was read that he had left everything but five dollars to his secretary. Naturally, the wife was furious. She drove to the establishment where the tombstone was being readied and ordered the inscription on her husband's monument changed. The engraver said, "I'm sorry, ma'am. You told me to inscribe 'Rest in Peace' on the stone, and that's what I did. I can't change it now, unless you want to buy a new stone." She thought for a moment.

Certainly, she didn't want to spend any more of her money. Finally, she said, "Right after 'Rest in Peace,' I want you to chisel in the words 'Till We Meet Again.'"

Yet getting revenge on the people who hurt you is a sad waste of precious time. It fills your heart with hatred, anger, and bitterness. Getting mad, seeking revenge, and getting even are all works of our flesh, and our flesh can only get us into more trouble. Getting revenge will never stop the bleeding. But it can lead to tragedy.

Disgruntled and Deadly

If we don't take immediate action to stop the bleeding, the continuing pain can easily warp our personality. Pain may not only kill the joy of living, but it may also take a deadlier turn. Consider the following excerpts from various newspapers in the United States.

- In March 1994, a disgruntled former employee walked into an electronics factory in Santa Fe Springs, California. He opened fire and shot three people working at their jobs.

- In February 1994, an employee of a Wendy's Old Fashioned Hamburgers restaurant in Tulsa, Oklahoma, entered the restaurant and shot and wounded three customers and three employees. He wanted a raise and a date with a girl who worked there.

- In January of the same year, four employees of a Taco Bell restaurant in Clarksville, Tennessee, were murdered in what appeared to be a gangland-style shooting. Authorities discovered the killings were committed by a former employee.

- A former employee killed four workers at a well-known pizza restaurant named Chuck E. Cheese in Aurora, Colorado, during the same month.

- Eric Houston was terminated in April 1992 from his job at Hewlett-Packard. He killed four people at his former high school in the town of Olivehurst, California. Apparently, he held them responsible for preparing him for such a "lousy job."

A 1992 Bureau of Labor Statistics study of fatal occupational injuries reported that homicide accounted for 17 percent of the 6083 work-related fatalities that year.[2] We can't help but wonder, *Does this have something to do with hurting people who never stopped the bleeding?*

The typical profile of a disgruntled worker is as follows:

white male
35 years or older
history of aggression
poor self-esteem
arsenal of weapons
record of labor-management disputes
history of drug/alcohol abuse
complains of work stress[3]

Dr. Michael Mantell is a clinical psychologist in private practice in San Diego. I first met Mike 14 years ago when he gave me an oral exam to see if I was fit to attend the police academy. Recently, I came across a copy of *USA Today* which included an article Mike had written about disgruntled employees. Mike is an expert police psychologist and is part of a national team of experts that immediately responds to tragedies such as mass shootings, wherever in the United States they might take place. Along with Steve Albrecht, Mike authored *Ticking Bombs: Defusing Violence in the Workplace*. Here are some of the book's conclusions:

> Reputation, credibility, efficiency, morale, productivity, absenteeism and employee turnover are the not-so-hidden costs of violence in the workplace for the employer.[4]

Some estimates place the dollar cost to corporate America for workplace violence at nearly $4.2 billion.[5]

The other victims—workers who themselves are not necessarily physically injured in the fury of a co-worker's rage and carnage—pay dearly in terms of job satisfaction, a sense of well-being and emotional scarring that often goes unseen for months or years, only erupting later in ways that are frequently misunderstood.[6]

Dr. Mantell says, "There is a practical, realistic and cost effective blueprint to deal with workplace violence"[7] and sees a solution for dealing with the warped personality of a "disgruntled employee." He says,

> Workplace violence won't go away because employers and their staff become better informed and aware of the causes and consequences of lethal and non-lethal forms of violence. It will go away by changing the make up of the American worker, manager and the work environment.
>
> This involves altering the nature of how the American family raises future employees and employers, the values it teaches, the methods of conflict resolution it promotes and the self-esteem it engenders in youngsters. It involves minimizing the amount of violence that our young people are exposed to in music, movies, magazines, television and in the culture in general.[8]

Now, I don't think we all will become serial killers because of divorce or abuse or loss of a job. But we all must look deeply inside ourselves and ask, Are we satisfied with our lives? Is there true peace in our hearts? Have we forgiven those who hurt us? Are there hurts inside us that we've never addressed, hurts that keep us from moving forward in life?

There definitely are side effects to our handling of hurts. Our lives and the people in them are affected, for good or ill, by our attention to or mishandling of our hurts. If we don't deal with our hurts properly, our personality can become warped, bringing a host of unforeseen—and possibly tragic—consequences.

How Are You Warped?

We're all warped differently. My warped personality shows up in ways typical of me. For instance, I catch myself standing at the door of the church on Sunday morning, usually in discomfort and pain. As I shake hands with people, I can become judgmental and look at situations with a cynical attitude. *Can't they see I'm hurting?* I wonder. *Can't they see how insensitive they are?* It's as if my pain dictates how I will respond to others.

It's not right. I have to be bigger than the pain. I am a minister of God's good news, and my life has to allow God's love to flow through me, no matter how I feel mentally or physically. Otherwise, I am a selfish servant. The apostle Paul told his young student Timothy, "Be ready in season and out of season." And yet that's how my warped personality often manifests itself.

Your warped personality probably has its own twist. I know whole families who are held hostage by "the family secret." It could be that one of the parents is an alcoholic. Or maybe years ago had molested or abused one of the children. Or perhaps there's a criminal past that no one is supposed to know about, or a sexual escapade with a coworker. Whatever it is, something is hidden, buried deep in the archives of family history. The wife or husband never discusses it. The child never confronts it. It's a phenomenally common masquerade inside the four walls of many an American home.

The pain may be hidden, but it never goes away. It shows up in the form of one family member attacking another. It's the sharp, jagged words used to cut down one person in front of others. It's there. Oh, it may not be a serial killer or mass murderer that we're talking about; it's you and me and everyday people who let the hurt warp our personality. We accept the discomfort. We live with a foggy mind and clouded head. We let numbness overshadow the raw feelings of being alive.

And it doesn't have to be that way.

Pain: A Part of Living

Pain is a part of living, and we must grow to accept that. It is an uncomfortable part of life, yet it's necessary. Imagine if you didn't have a nervous system. You would never know if you were shot in the leg or if you had cut your hand with a knife. Pain is a warning system. When our body is in trouble—when it's been hurt or injured—pain sounds the alarm. Our healing process kicks in and begins to race to the scene of the hurt.

If our body has been invaded by a virus or bacteria, the brain receives the latest update from the blood system and starts creating antibodies to attack the infection. Our muscles and ligaments, along with our skeletal system, send a message via the nervous system that something is wrong, that part of our body needs extra attention.

Then the brain alerts the affected parts of our body to prepare for shock. Adrenaline is released, muscles tense up or relax, the heart starts pumping faster, and the body's defense mechanisms go into motion. Pain was the alarm that set it all off.

Now, though our bodies are wonderfully made and in many instances heal themselves, they often (and more than likely) need to have the injury bound up and the wound dressed.

What is true in the physical realm is also true in the emotional realm. Hurt is a warning system that something is not right. Something has attacked our well-being. There has been an intrusion by friend or foe who has verbally or physically hurt us. Life situations have stacked up so much that we are overstressed and cannot cope. All of these symptoms form part of a warning system which God designed within us so we could recheck our course and make sure that we are heading in the right direction.

Whenever I'm really hurting, I try hard to remember that if I were not feeling pain, I would probably be dead. And I want to live. It is wonderful to be alive; every day is a new adventure, like a clean sheet of paper ready to be filled in, line by line. I learned years ago that my life was so messed up that the pages were filled with garbage. I knew I needed a fresh beginning. I had too many debts from yesterday; too many people I upset at the party over the weekend; too many things left undone at work. Perhaps you know the feeling: helpless and hopeless.

I'm sure that's why alcohol and drugs sell so well. They help people cover the pain that comes with confusion and failure. That's where we begin to get so deep in our depression that life truly becomes warped for us. Oh, most of us don't blow up a building or rob a bank. We don't go loony and harm other people. We simply allow our minds to breed a warped sense of view.

The fruit of that worldview shows up in many ways. Missed appointments. Bounced checks. Fights with our loved ones. Arriving late to work. Drinking excessively or pill-taking. Friendships fall apart. You get the point.

Now, here is the good news. Life does not need to continue like this. You may think, *Right, Mike. Easy for you to say. You don't know what it's like.* Actually, I do know what it's like. For 26 years, I struggled terribly with life (you'll learn more about that as this book progresses). I never knew there was a way out of the darkness, a way that could replace my confusion with clarity, my despair with great hope. Please let me help you find the secrets to life that you, too, may have spent years looking for.

We are told that King Solomon was the wisest man who ever lived. In the first six chapters of the book of Proverbs, Solomon often repeats to his son, "If you will listen to my words and take heed to them, you will do well." Now, no way am I saying that I have the wisdom of King Solomon, but I am honestly asking you to listen to me, because I have been where you are in your hurt. In the second half of my life I have seen God take me from the bottom of the trash heap, clean me up, and set me on my own two feet. Not only did He stand me up, but He also has given me a fairly productive life.

I know life can hurt. I know life can be unjust and unfair. Nevertheless, it can also bring great joy and a tremendous challenge. Join me and see how you can leave behind that fun-house-mirror image of yourself. Learn how you, too, can gain a clear vision for life and leave behind the old, warped outlook.

A Puzzling Scripture

Often we blame God for the bad things that come into our lives. We should instead try to look at life from a broader perspective. A key element of leaving behind a warped outlook is to realize there is an intelligent, sinister force working overtime to find which buttons to push in your life to destroy you. That sinister force is the devil. He hates you with a passion. When you are hurting, he's happy. How he must laugh when he can get human beings to destroy themselves! Jesus called him a "murderer from the beginning," and Peter tells us he roams the earth, looking for people to destroy.

I don't have any trouble at all understanding the Bible's warnings about the devil. I know firsthand how he loves to cause hurt, pain, and suffering. Yet another portion of Scripture puzzled me for years. It just didn't seem to make sense to me. Hosea 6:1-3 (KJV) says,

> Come, and let us return unto the LORD: for he hath torn, and he will heal us; he hath smitten, and he will bind us up. After two days will he revive us: in the third day he will raise us up, and we shall live in his sight. Then shall we know, if we follow on to know the LORD: his going forth is prepared as the morning; and he shall come unto us as the rain, as the latter and former rain unto the earth.

It always stumped me why it says, "For he hath torn, and he will heal us; he hath smitten, and he will bind us up." Then one day I realized that not all hurt is from the devil. God may allow pain to come into our lives for a purpose. Notice that Hosea says if God has torn, *He will heal*. The Scripture says, "He hath smitten," but note it also says, "*He will bind us up.*"

Great are the mysteries of godliness. We can't figure everything out that God does or allows. We do know, of course, that "all things work together for good" (Romans 8:28). Everything isn't guaranteed to be good, but the circumstances somehow will gel together for good—no matter how difficult the circumstances may be.

A Disturbing Dream

A number of years ago I awoke early one morning from an unusual dream that made no sense at all. Yet the dream was as vivid as a motion picture in a downtown theater. In it I was running from a motorcycle gang. The gang had been bullying me and threatened to kill me. I ran away and hid in a yard behind some shrubs close to the house.

Soon I heard the sound of a motorcycle chugging slowly up the street near me, the biker coasting past my hiding place. He was bigger than me and would have made a formidable foe. He wore a large Nazi army helmet and a thick, bulky jacket. As he pulled into the backyard where I was hiding, suddenly his motorcycle slid out from underneath him in the wet grass. I knew this was my chance.

I picked up a huge stick to hit him from behind. Just as I lifted the club over my head to bring it down on his neck, he turned and stared me directly in the eyes. I was shocked, amazed, dumbfounded—I was looking into the eyes of my very own pastor, Chuck Smith.

At that moment I woke up. I couldn't believe such a scene had filled my mind. I took a shower, and still it replayed in my thoughts. It was 7:30 A.M. and I told Sandy that I was driving from San Diego to Pastor Chuck's office to see him. I explained the dream to her, which puzzled her, too.

For the next hour and a half, I drove north and prayed for clarity and understanding. Chuck is one of the busiest men in the country, and to walk in unannounced is not my style. Yet I knew the dream meant *something*. When I arrived in Costa Mesa, Chuck was viewing a movie about our friend Raul Ries. As usual, he was very cordial, but he really didn't have time to see me because he was already one hour late to a speaking engagement. Still, I needed to tell him the dream. I asked him to give me a moment. As I described the dream, I did not know its interpretation. Even if it had a spiritual connotation, it was beyond me.

But when I got to the part about the big biker turning around and looking me in the face—and the biker was

Chuck—the meaning came to me. Chuck was being made to look like something he wasn't. His enemies were hitting him while he was down. Yet he remained humble and calm, refusing to fight back or assail his attackers. Then Hosea 6 came to me. The Lord wanted to encourage Chuck that God was in control, no matter what anyone said, thought, or did to him. God would bind up and heal.

Later I found out there truly were detractors who had taken advantage of this wonderful man, hurting him and damaging the church. They were painting a picture of him that was not true.

What About You?

Is it possible that such a scenario echoes your own situation? Someone has deliberately hurt you, and you're defenseless. You're in pain, and you don't know what to do. If that describes your plight—or even if you're hurting for some other reason—let this book be an encouragement to you. Allow the love of God to work through your heart this very moment. He has allowed this pain to come your way, and He has promised to bind you up and heal you. Life is so tough at times. Yet when the pain is the sharpest, the suffering the deepest, that is where God comes in and shows us His strength and His power.

Open your heart right now to the Lord and allow Him to stanch the bleeding. Remember, pain exists to remind us that we are still alive. The discomfort tells us there is a problem which needs to be fixed. Don't ever forget that there is a real devil who delights in your misery. On the other hand, never lose sight that there is an omnipotent God full of love and compassion for you and your loved ones. He has a personal plan for your life. While His plan may not always be your plan, His plan will conclude with a binding up. It will end with healing. Ultimately, it will end in heaven with eternal healing.

God is the One who will stop your bleeding. We may not know the "what abouts" or "whys" of God—God's ways are not our ways—but we do know He is a God of love. Our part is to trust, obey, and believe. He will do the rest. God has a divine purpose in all of this. So give Him a chance. After all, He has given you many.

2

Death,
The Ultimate Hurt

—The Tender Touch of God—

Youngsters wrote the following two letters to God. What simplicity and candor little ones have!

> Dear God, What is it like to die? I just want to know. I don't want to do it.
>
> Michael

> Dear Lord, My grandma just went to heaven. Please take care of her. Her name is Grandma.
>
> Your Christian, Paul
> (age 7, Cincinnati)[1]

Death is so mysterious to us—especially when it comes unexpectedly. It is painful enough when someone we love is ill or hospitalized and we know that there is a good chance he or she may die. But when the death is unexpected, it has the power to traumatize those who knew and loved the deceased.

This type of pain can continue literally for years. I know. That's what it did with me.

Don't Ever Say That Again!

I will never forget the day I heard the news. It was August 19, 1959—a warm, clear, sunny summer day. And it brought a hurricane of hurt.

I had just been involved in a fistfight. Mike MacIntosh, a 145 pounder, took on Bo Welch and all of his 245 pounds. The two of us had exchanged words in the school hallway, but I never dreamed the "big fella" would take me up on my challenge. Of course, it was not an even match. I think an angel kept me from being pulverized. A crowd surrounded us as we circled each other—Bo keeping away from me because I was throwing some good punches; me keeping away from Bo because, as a wrestler, I knew that once he got hold of me, I was done for.

In the middle of our fight, a little old lady came walking down the street and yelled, "Hey, you big bully, why don't you pick on somebody your own size?" For some reason we quit fighting, shook hands, said our apologies, and the crowd split. Strange thing, I looked at my watch and noted the exact time. I found out later that my mom also remembers looking at the clock at precisely the same time. When I returned home, I saw the clock there also had stopped at precisely the same hour. Very strange.

After Mom returned home from work, I walked to the store with a friend. On the return trip, a friend of my oldest brother pulled up alongside the curb and told us to get in. We did so, but something on the driver's face told me something was wrong.

"What's the matter?" I asked.

"Is your mother home?" she replied.

"Yes, but what's wrong?"

"Wait until we get to your house and I'll tell you."

"No! Tell me now—what is the matter?"

Even after all these years, I can still see the scene as clearly as if it were playing on a tape in the VCR. I can still see Penny Williamson looking into my face and saying, "Your brother David was killed in an automobile accident two hours ago."

"That's a lie!" I raged. "Don't ever say anything like that again!" But my anger was misdirected; Penny was telling the awful truth. David had been a passenger in a coworker's new 1959 Volvo, taking a quick ride before his afternoon shift began at work. When the driver sped across some railroad tracks at more than 70 miles per hour, his vehicle spun out of control and slammed into a telephone pole on a country road just outside Sacramento. David was killed instantly.

We drove the rest of the way home in silence. When we arrived, Penny went in with me and asked me to put on a pot of coffee; then she would tell my mom. Things went faster than anticipated, however. I knew instantly when my mother heard the news, for a scream went up from the living room of our little two-bedroom apartment. I've never heard such a scream since, nor do I ever want to hear it again. It was the wail of a mother who has just learned of the death of one of her dear children.

It took me 20 years to finally let loose of the hurt I felt when I learned my brother was dead. I can remember so clearly standing with my mother beside David's open coffin in the funeral home. I just would not let myself believe that he had died. He was only 26, married, and had an infant son. This had to be a bad joke.

The death of anyone in your family is horrible at any age; but if death knocks at your door during the frustrating, formative teens, it can leave deep, ugly scars. The hurt caused by my own brother's death cut so deeply that it warped my personality for two decades. I trace ten years of hard drinking to this loss. I decided to cover the hurt. I became the life of the party, a regular party animal. I wandered aimlessly through two years of high school, then dropped out.

Because I didn't know how to "stop the bleeding," the pain killed my joy of living and warped my personality. The sad thing is that Mom, my brother Kent, and I were all suffering, yet none of us knew how to talk about it or where to turn for help. We didn't stop the bleeding, and we all paid the price for many years to come.

When Death Comes Knocking

How we handle death can either shape our destiny in a negative way or allow us to stop the bleeding and go forward. Consider three moving incidents from my own experience:

- A very dear friend asked me to officiate at the funeral service of her mother, to whom she was very close. Only a few weeks after her mother had been diagnosed with a brain tumor, she was dead, leaving a son about 12 years younger than my friend. The little boy knew only that his mommy was sick and had to go to the hospital. When the family arrived at the mortuary, somehow the little boy wandered into the chapel and saw his mother's open coffin. His sister and father didn't know he was there. He walked up to the coffin and for the first time realized his mother was dead. He sobbed and sobbed. When I saw what

36

was happening, I ran over to him, wrapped my arms around him, and turned him away from the coffin. He was devastated. What an awful way to learn of your mother's death!

- A young man in his twenties committed suicide—yet another victim of illicit drugs. He left behind three small children. His wife, also a lost soul, was unable to mother their three children, so county authorities sent them to live with three separate families. At his daddy's funeral service, the four-year-old son came running back to the grave side where the coffin was ready to be lowered into the ground. The little guy put his hand on the coffin and said, "Daddy! Daddy! Come out of the box!" Then he turned to me, looked up at my six-foot frame, and pleaded, "I want my daddy. Can't you open the box and get my daddy for me?"

- In San Diego a man tried to kill his wife and two children. Finally, he took the knife, looked at his nine-year-old son, and said, "You're to blame for all of this. Someday you will understand." Then he plunged the knife into his own heart and died in front of his children. When the boy's uncle told me this story five days after it had occurred, I immediately asked if I could talk with the boy. When the uncle brought the children to church, I sat with the boy and told him that sometimes big people are sick and take the wrong medicine that often makes them do and say things they don't mean to do or say. I wanted him to know that all of the ugliness that had happened in his family that week was not his fault. We prayed together, and I continue to pray that the Holy Spirit will erase the ugliness from that tender little soul.

I have found that funeral services are often a time for people to come to grips with the "ultimate pain." A great emotional release can take place when a loved one has finally been laid to rest. As a minister, I have marveled at the work that can be accomplished at a funeral service. I also marvel at the gaping wound that remains open for many people.

Since I, too, have lost loved ones and family members, I always try to choose my words carefully during these services. In addition, I have always made it a matter of protocol to be the last one standing beside the coffin and grave side. The last memory I want to leave is that a minister of God was there from start to finish. It is here, at the funeral and grave side, that people can grasp the important issues of life and death. When they go home and sit alone, the healing process can be expedited if the biblical truths of life and death have been heard and grasped at the memorial service.

On the other hand, I have presided at other services which left a sorrowful memory. I can tell you one thing for sure: Funerals for Christians are much easier to officiate than services for nonbelievers. The Christian has hope; the nonbeliever has none. Even the spirit and the mood of the audience is different. That conviction was brought home to me forcefully in the spring of 1995.

Eleven Funerals in Ten Days

It was a warm spring Wednesday morning on April 19, 1995, when an explosion rocked the Alfred P. Murrah Federal Building in Oklahoma City, Oklahoma. At 9:02 A.M., a powerful blast toppled nine stories of concrete and marble, instantly crushing scores of innocent victims inside. Within moments, television screens across the country filled with scenes of bleeding survivors and bodies being carried from the rubble. The physical and emotional pain went beyond anything we could have imagined.

Months later, victims' families and friends were still suffering from the trauma of this atrocity. One hundred sixty-nine people eventually lost their lives in the explosion, including 19 children. Another 614 people were known to be injured. Authorities have no count on the number of people who might have been vaporized from the blast—people on the sidewalk, getting into or out of automobiles, or entering or leaving the building.

Oklahoma City held scores of funeral services over the days that followed the bombing. The January 1996 issue of *Life* magazine quoted a local man who attended 11 funerals in 10 days. Even then, he despaired because he couldn't attend services for every friend he had lost.

Since I have been involved in chaplaincy programs with law-enforcement officials for many years, I had a tremendous personal concern for the federal agents and law-enforcement officers who worked at the scene of the tragedy. I called a friend who had been a deputy director in the FBI and let him know I was available to help; he made a few calls to his contacts. I also got letters of introduction from the San Diego chief of police and San Diego County sheriff. My heart was heavy knowing what the men and women in the law-enforcement agencies would have to see, hear and do in cleaning up the rubble. I left for Oklahoma City and, after introducing myself to local authorities, began to talk with those on the scene and listen carefully to their hurts. I noticed immediately several common denominators.

First, it was almost impossible for these dedicated workers to process the enormity of the blast and the destruction it had caused.

Second, the death of innocent children was excruciatingly difficult on those charged with carrying their bodies out of the rubble.

Third, most of the federal workers and law-enforcement personnel on the scene lost friends and coworkers in the blast. One federal agent told me that five minutes prior to the explosion, he had been on the phone to a man he had known for years; they had worked together on several cases. That man was killed in the blast. The realization that it was the last time he would ever speak to his friend was simply too much to bear. As we stood in the rain and tried to put his hurt into perspective, exhaustion was etched into this officer's face; he had been up for more than 31 hours without sleep when we talked.

Another evening a different officer was helping to extract bodies from the debris when he discovered a very close friend was the object of the search. It was pitiful to watch his reaction. In the few moments we talked, he went from remorse, hurt, and sadness, to deep anger. "I hate this building," he said ferociously.

What do you say to someone in such a circumstance? This man was truly bleeding from the soul. While kind words and simple compassion for his hurt could begin to stop his bleeding, his hurt was extremely deep, and I knew it would be impossible to see a complete healing in only a few moments of conversation. Yet that doesn't mean that nothing could be accomplished through compassionate dialogue.

I realized it was important to remember what King Solomon said: "A soft answer turns away wrath, but a harsh word stirs up anger" (Proverbs 15:1). It would have been easy to vent my anger and frustrations over the ugliness of the situation. By doing so, I might have gained a sympathetic ear or two from those standing by—but my calling was higher than that. This suffering man needed soft, biblical words. I wanted to stop the bleeding, and soft words of compassion were exactly what he needed. I knew some of the best are found in Psalm 23.

Responding to the Ultimate Hurt

One of the most beloved sections of the Old Testament is Psalms. Most of the 150 psalms were penned by King David of Israel, and they leave hardly a stone unturned regarding man and his suffering, hurt, and pain. The great thing about these writings is that they all point to God for the resolution of our hurts.

Consider Psalm 23. This psalm deals with the fears of death in the context of faith and trust in God. Take the time to slowly read through these six short verses. Savor the message like a soothing ointment:

> The LORD is my shepherd; I shall not want. He makes me to lie down in green pastures; He leads me beside the still waters. He restores my soul; He leads me in the paths of righteousness for His name's sake. Yea, though I walk through the valley of the shadow of death, I will fear no evil; for You are with me; Your rod and Your staff, they comfort me. You prepare a table before me in the presence of my enemies; You anoint my head with oil; my cup runs over. Surely goodness and mercy shall follow me all the days of my life; and I will dwell in the house of the LORD forever.

For the believer, this psalm is filled with comfort and hope. It is almost as if this psalm were written specifically to help stop the bleeding of the ultimate hurt.

1. *The Lord is my shepherd; I shall not want.*

When David penned the twenty-third psalm, he was writing from very personal experience as a shepherd. His father, Jesse, had owned many sheep, and from his youth, David had helped his father and brothers take care of the flocks.

We know from Scripture that David was a faithful and courageous servant for his father. David had seen God work in defending the defenseless. He knew from personal experience that God would protect His own. David knew how a loving shepherd looked after his sheep, so it was natural for him to think of the Lord as his Shepherd. He knew that God was a loving God, and that, therefore, he should never worry about his physical or emotional needs. God was in control, and David would trust Him.

This lesson is just as important for us as it was for David. When hurt comes our way, we must trust God. He is the Shepherd of our souls, and He knows what's best for us. It's only natural for us to want immediate relief or deliverance from our troubles. But look closely at David's words. "I shall *not* want," he says. As one of God's sheep, David says, we shall never want. Why not? Because everything we need is in our supply house; all of the cupboards and shelves are full.

2. He makes me to lie down in green pastures; He leads me beside the still waters.

A good shepherd will cause his sheep to find rest. Notice: David says, "He [God] *makes*." Often our lives are so rushed we don't take the time to rest. The Lord will help us to rest—and force us, if necessary—in times of hurt and pain.

A good shepherd is interested not only in what his sheep do, but also where they do it. Green pastures are not only the right place for sheep to feast, but also the best place for them. Hired hands usually aren't concerned if the sheep are given the best. The sheep don't belong to them; to them, it's "only a job."

Contrastively, the Lord does what any good shepherd does: He finds the best spot for us. It's our job simply to trust Him when the ultimate pain strikes. He will take care of us even if we feel disoriented, confused, stymied, or lost.

David next reminds us that sheep are timid and shy creatures. They are one of the few animals in the food chain that are completely vulnerable to predators. Sheep have no defensive capabilities. No claws or sharp teeth. No poison or venom. No bulging muscles. Not even a good growl or menacing look. Because of this, sheep are easy to spook.

Sheep can't easily relax, let alone lie down, near any kind of loud, swirling waters. It is just too unsettling. This is why the good shepherd finds green pastures beside "still waters." He wants them to relax and let him provide all they need.

The Lord does the same thing for us. Hurt causes turmoil and upsets our balance. It puts us off guard, as if we are being tossed about in the rapids during a whitewater rafting trip. Hurt and pain can cause us to feel that we are "up a creek without a paddle."

That is why David reminds us that our Good Shepherd will lead us by the still waters. Don't worry, the Lord is looking after you and will provide the peace you need—even during the ultimate hurt.

3. *He restores my soul; He leads me in the paths of righteousness for His name's sake.*

Here David brings real comfort to our hearts. "He restores [our] soul." The soul is our very being, our character, our personality. The Greeks defined it as the seat of human feelings, desires, affections, and aversions. From the Greek word translated "soul," we get our word *psyche* and all its derivatives, including *psychology, psychiatry*, etc.

Since God created your soul, He knows exactly how to restore it. Let Him do what He does best. The ultimate hurt seems as if it will never go away, but have patience; the Lord is working on your behalf.

Remember: He watched His only begotten Son die on the cross for the sins of the world, both yours and mine. He knows what you are going through. Jesus Himself understands this very well. It was He who said, "I am the good shepherd: the good shepherd giveth his life for the sheep. . . . I am the good shepherd, and know my sheep, and am known of mine" (John 10:11,14 KJV).

The New Testament insists that Jesus really understands our hurts and pain. He knows what suffering is like more thoroughly than any of us possibly could. The book of Hebrews says:

> Seeing then that we have a great high priest, that is passed into the heavens, Jesus the Son of God, let us hold fast our profession.
> For we have not an high priest which cannot be touched with the feeling of our infirmities; but was in all points tempted like as we are, yet without sin. Let us therefore come boldly unto the throne of grace, that we may obtain mercy, and find grace to help in time of need (Hebrews 4:14-16 KJV).

Now can you see why He is able to help you through this terrible, trying time? As they say on the street, "Been there! Done that!" He knows, so trust Him. He will "restore your soul."

It may seem impossible that the ultimate hurt will ever go away, but it will. Trust Him. Search the Scriptures. Find your story in the Psalms and let it speak to you to heal your wound. The Psalms were written from the heart and most are based on painful experiences—painful life experiences like yours and mine.

Yet all of them show that God is ultimately in charge and that He will bring victory to His children. "In all these things we are more than conquerors through him that loved us," Paul writes in Romans 8:37 (KJV).

So rest in the Lord. Trust in Him. The Lord is so good. He's waiting for you right now. Talk with Him and listen to His small, still voice. He will stop the bleeding and bring you tremendous peace.

Isaiah says, "But they that wait upon the LORD shall renew their strength; they shall mount up with wings as eagles; they shall run, and not be weary; and they shall walk, and not faint" (Isaiah 40:31 KJV). The road might look long and lonely before you, but help is here. Look for the God of heaven and earth to take control. The future may seem like a long, long dark tunnel, and you don't know if, you'll be able to go on; but you will. Your strength will return, and you will find a freshness and newness to life. You will once again be vibrant. And above all, you will be able to help other people who are suffering the same kinds of hurts that have come upon you.

Healing After 20 Years

At the beginning of this chapter I described the death of my brother David, and how I carried the hurt of his death with me for two decades until at last God brought peace to my heart. How did God heal this deep, cutting hurt? As I said, it took 20 years. During the last five of those years, I entered the ministry. Again, God's plan was brilliant. He knew the nightmares I had concerning my brother. He knew the lonely nights in bars I had spent "crying in my beer"—so many beers that I forgot why I cried.

Although I didn't fully recognize it at the time, buried with my hurt was intense anger and bitterness against God. Why would a loving God allow such a tragedy to happen? My brother had a wife and a new baby boy. Why would God allow this? Why would He allow my mother to feel such excruciating pain? It wasn't fair. Life was always dumping on us, and no one was there to help.

I had turned to God in junior high school, but I turned from God in high school. A good amount of my hurt was anger and bitterness against the God who had let me down, who had failed to live up to my expectations. That's why it took so long for me to be healed of that ultimate pain of losing the brother I so dearly loved.

My own healing finally began one day as I officiated at the funeral of a 17-year-old who had died from an overdose of drugs and alcohol at a party. His parents were ashamed of the incident and devastated that they could have lost their son in such a manner. They told their son's high school friends that he had suffered heart failure (which was partially true, because his heart did actually fail because of the overdose).

The chapel was standing room only; this good-looking kid was very popular. Some music was played, his girlfriend read a poem, then his friends came to the microphone and said nice words about their departed buddy.

Finally, I got up and spoke about eternal life and the value of trusting in God. I also gave an opportunity for people to make a commitment to Jesus. Then, as I stood by the open casket and everyone filed past in a reverent and orderly manner, it hit me. The mother and father came and stood all alone, weeping and looking down into the bloodless face of the young man they had raised. I knew the pain they were feeling and understood their grief. Twenty years earlier I had been in that same position.

In fact, every time in my 25 years of ministry when I have stood beside deathbeds, caskets, and graves I have remembered the open casket of my brother and the tears of his wife, my mother, my brother Kent, and myself. I remember the doctor giving us some medication to cushion the blow. I recall how the staff where my mother worked bought her new tires, tuned her car, filled the tank, and took up a collection so two teenaged brothers could drive from Portland, Oregon, to Sacramento, California, with their bereaved mother.

As I stood with that mother and father some 20 years later, God brought healing to me concerning David's death. He showed me that, as a minister, my personal hurt and pain allows me to help more people. I am now able to say the kind words and offer the gentle remarks that I hoped the minister had said to my widowed sister-in-law two decades ago. I can put my arm around the shoulders of brothers standing in the chapel and explain that God will use even this for good. I know when a single parent is burying her only child that she needs someone to be there for her, to listen to her anguish, to comfort and reassure her that she will make it through this terrible storm. It is through my own pain that I am able to help others through their pain.

Now that I see how God can use this tragedy for His glory, I have found a great peace and a great healing. That which I feared so much for so many years I no longer fear. As Paul the apostle proclaimed: "Oh death, where is thy sting? O grave, where is thy victory?" (1 Corinthians 15:55 KJV).

Like Paul, I too shout for joy. For you see, the "ultimate pain" is not really ultimate at all. It hurts terribly and it's very real, but it's far from ultimate. The grace and mercy and love of the Great Shepherd see to that.

While it's true (as the psalmist says) that death is a dark, shadowy valley, for the believer that valley always leads to the kingdom of light—and to the loving Father in whom "is no variation or shadow of turning" (James 1:17).

And there's nothing more ultimate than that.

3

Accidents Ahead

The Tender Touch of God

In the last chapter I mentioned that for many years I have served as a police chaplain. I consider it one of the great privileges of my life. My main mission is to the officers and their families. I have performed funeral services and weddings, counseled, and befriended many officers over the years. This always has been a challenging and fulfilling experience.

San Diego is the sixth-largest city in America. Beyond any doubt, it has more than its share of crime. The stress levels can grow very high for the personnel. This is where the chaplain can be most helpful. No part of the job is more fulfilling than to ride along with officers on their ten-hour work shifts. During these times I am able to identify with the officers and also let them get to know me. I always stay out of the way, but more times than not I have been asked to assist in one way or another.

Trauma at a Corner Crossing

One summer evening I was riding along with the San Diego police; it was the second watch in a rough part of town. My partner had taken a "code 7" (lunch break). It was around 9 P.M., and she hadn't had a second to rest since she'd hit the streets six hours earlier. It was one of those days when a lot of people decided they didn't want to "love their brother." As we finished our meal and paid the bill, a call came concerning a vehicle and pedestrian accident less than one mile from our location.

When we arrived, we saw an ugly scene.

Another officer who had arrived before us was bending over an elderly woman's body. A stream of blood flowed from her neck down the hill toward us. She had been struck in the crosswalk while proceeding against the wait sign. After we put out road flares and redirected traffic, witnesses told us the woman had been in the corner bar, drinking. She was killed instantly.

The driver of the car which hit her was a young women in her mid-twenties. She had just left a friend's house and was on her way home when the accident occurred. She had turned the corner and begun to climb the short hill, the green light in her favor. The last thing she remembered was the woman's face smashing through her windshield. She slammed on her brakes and stopped immediately, catapulting the victim off the windshield and onto the pavement.

This young lady was so traumatized that all she could do was scream and sob convulsively. As the officer did her duties, I tried to help the driver calm down. She collapsed on the sidewalk.

Only after the arrival of the young woman's parents could we help her to the patrol car. Her mom and dad accompanied her to the emergency room at a local hospital where she was treated for shock and sedated. Then she was released to her parents' care and taken home.

I felt sure this young woman would need follow-up to help her cope with the accident, even though she was innocent of any wrongdoing. I gave my police chaplain business card to her parents and told them I was available to help in any manner they saw fit. If their daughter would like to talk about the tragedy, I would be available. I never heard a word from that young woman or her family until almost one year later.

One Sunday evening I was teaching a Bible study at our church when two women approached me with the most incredible story. One asked if we had ever met before; my voice sounded familiar to her, even though she had never been to the church. Then I recognized her: She was the woman driving the car months earlier. Her friend attended our church and had invited her to visit.

It turned out that since the accident, the driver had been enduring much grief and suffering, yet didn't know where to turn. About six months after the wreck, she called a longtime girlfriend. She figured if anyone could help, it would be her. When she asked for her friend, she was told no one by that name lived there. But after both parties hung up, the young woman who made that statement thought, *How stupid of me. That was my sister's name until she got married and moved out.* Then she prayed and asked the Lord to have that person call back if it was important.

At that exact moment the troubled young woman was thinking that she must have dialed the number incorrectly, so she re-dialed. This time the voice on the other end told her that her sister used to live there, and that was her name. So it was the right number after all! When the two women exchanged names, they immediately recognized each other. "Where is your sister now?" asked the first woman. "I am in big trouble, and I need her to help me." The young woman from our church explained that her sister had married a young man who had just been discharged from the Navy. This seemed unbelievable to the lady looking for help. "Your sister and boyfriend like to party too much. How could they settle down and marry? They were both the single type."

The woman then explained that her sister and boyfriend grew tired of the party life and decided to go to church one Sunday. It was there that they learned of God's great love for them, and they both asked God to come into their lives and change them. They became Christians and immediately dropped the party scene, realized how much they loved each other, decided to marry, and settled down.

"What does all of that mean?" the troubled young woman asked. Then she began to spill her guts over the phone. At that point the invitation came for her to attend church. She gave her heart to the Lord and immediately found the peace she had so desperately sought. On the Sunday evening I heard this story, she had come to Horizon Christian Fellowship with her new friend.

Only after the evening service did it dawn on her that I was the police chaplain at the scene of the accident. The wreck had put her in such a state of shock that she didn't know who I was or that I had helped her. She remembered only my voice—a voice that had broken through the thick fog of adrenaline and trauma. All through the Bible study her mind was trying to recognize the voice. How grateful we both were when she realized that God had been with her both during and after the accident!

They Happen to Everyone

Accidents happen to all of us. They do not have to be automobile collisions or something tragic; an accident is merely "an unexpected, undesirable event." Sometimes we use the term to refer to an unforeseen-but-harmless incident—perhaps we chose to shop at a certain store but ended up at another one "by accident." Or maybe it was "by accident" that we went to the wrong party and the police arrested us.

However we view an accident, in each case it is a disruption of our plans. Often these disruptions bring terrible hurt, turmoil, and pain into our lives.

Two weeks ago, Sandy was driving on the freeway. The driver of a large truck did not see her when he decided to switch lanes and caused an accident. Fortunately, no one was hurt (but the truck severely damaged her car). Yesterday, Sandy took my car shopping and, in trying to avoid an oncoming car, by accident pulled too close to the wall, damaging the rear door. Now, when Sandy went shopping she had no intention to dent the car. It was an accident, and accidents cause frustration and anxiety.

I guess we can raise the question, Are there really accidents in God's plan? The apostle Paul didn't seem to think so. In Romans 8:28 he wrote, "We know that all things work together for good to those who love God, to those who are the called according to His purpose." Please notice that Paul doesn't state that all things are good; heaven knows that accidents aren't good. Instead, he wrote, "All things work together *for* good."

Have you been involved in an accident that has crippled your ability to move on or has eroded your faith in God? Please, don't let it continue to injure you; instead, let it be an opportunity for you to stop the bleeding in your life. The accident itself is never good, but it can work together for good if God is at the helm—just as the Lord put me on the scene for a tragic event one balmy summer night a year ago. He has His angels and His people around you, too. Even when it doesn't seem as if He does.

Triple Tragedy

Caroline was 19 years old—a tall, slender, pretty young woman filled with love for her boyfriend. The two had planned their wedding for June 4. You can imagine the excitement and joy in the heart of this young bride-to-be, filled with the giddy expectations we would all share at a time like this.

One night the phone rang at the farmhouse where Caroline lived. It was Memorial Day, a happy time for everyone in the small Kansas farming community. The city park's band shell had been filled with festive music, and the lawns of many homes overflowed with water from the sprinklers the children had spent the afternoon running through. When Caroline answered the phone, the editor of the local newspaper told her he had been driving home and had come upon an automobile accident. Apparently, a 17-year-old boy had been drinking and haphazardly made a left turn in front of an oncoming car. The driver and the passenger in that car were both in critical condition and had been taken to the local hospital. The editor told her the two passengers were her brother and fiancé.

Caroline rushed to the hospital in time to see them both alive—but their injuries were so severe that both died within two hours. Caroline was devastated.

Her fiancé had been from Toronto, Canada. After the funeral for her brother, she boarded a plane carrying the remains of her fiancé and flew to his services. Upon arriving at the terminal in Toronto, she was greeted by what was to have been her mother-in-law and other in-laws. All were weeping inconsolably. They explained that the death of her fiancé so shocked the young man's father that he suffered a heart attack and died the next day. So it was that on June 4—the day she was to be married—Caroline buried her brother, her fiancé, and her intended father-in-law. She called it a "triple tragedy."

I recently met Caroline while preaching in a local crusade. Her story reminded me that tragedy and accidents don't happen only in "the big city"; they also occur "down on the farm." It had been 22 years since the incident. As she recounted the story, I could still see the hurt in her eyes and hear the agony in this now 41-year-old woman's heart and soul. "How did you cope with such deep pain?" I asked. She said she tried to run from it and cover it up. She began a masquerade in her soul, so she didn't have to face the tragedy. She also began to make decisions based unknowingly on the hurt caused by this triple tragedy—decisions that would cause her even more grief.

After a couple years living as a recluse, she began to date once more. She trusted an older man and married him—something she felt would heal her. After all, he was a minister. She didn't know he had never committed himself to God, and therefore could not commit himself to her.

At the age of 24, she found out she was going to have her first child. It was then she discovered that her husband was being unfaithful. After being exposed, he left his church, abandoned his pregnant wife—along with all the debts associated with their new marriage—and slipped out of town by night, not to be heard from again until a year or two later. A divorce was the final solution.

I asked Caroline if she had ever talked to the young man responsible for the fatal accident. "No," she replied, even though his parents still lived in the same farmhouse they occupied 22 years ago. I asked Caroline if she ever talked to his parents. When there was a pause, I knew there was more to this story. You see, Caroline lives quite near this couple. Every day she passes that farmhouse, always remembering the "triple tragedy."

In trying to help this lovely lady find peace, I suggested she stop at that house, walk up to the porch, and knock on the door. It is more than likely that this dear mother and father have felt pain and hurt, just like Caroline. It is probable that their son still carries a tremendous amount of guilt and pain. Though it may be buried or masked, it has probably haunted this young man for more than two decades.

At the time Caroline told me her story, I was a guest of several local churches in her county. One of my best friends, Paul Clark, had been invited to sing during the evening gatherings in the city park. Paul had been quietly standing beside us, listening to this tragic story. When I finished talking, Paul said, "I remember that night 22 years ago on Memorial Day. I was standing right here at the band shell, singing and playing my guitar. Police and ambulance sirens were blaring out toward the highway. Later we were told that a terrible automobile accident had occurred and that someone had been killed."

The Old Testament says, "at the mouth of two witnesses, or at the mouth of three witnesses, shall the matter be established" (Deuteronomy 19:15 KJV). In this case, God had waited 22 years to bring Paul Clark and myself to Caroline's side to encourage her, as if we were two witnesses who could establish in her mind that she could be released from her deep pain.

Like Caroline, we too can mistakenly avoid working through tough situations, only to face tougher situations later on. If you want to stop the bleeding that has come to you through an accident, you must first face the problem. It may seem impossible to do so, but if God is at your side, it's more than possible; it's an opportunity to discover His loving, healing hands. And when accidents strike, that's what we need more than anything else.

Wet, Wild, and Scary

One of my all-time best friends is Dr. Sherwood Elliot Wirt. He and his lovely wife, Ruth, are always an inspiration to me by their commitment to the Christian faith and their zest for life. I feel as if I've had the wonderful privilege of being adopted by this loving, gentle giant. Woody (as he is called by friends), holds the elaborate title of editor emeritus of *Decision* magazine. That's a complex way of saying that he helped Billy Graham launch a dream of his.

That dream was to create a magazine which would encourage Christians, stimulate evangelism, highlight the productive work of the Billy Graham Evangelistic Association—and above all, preach the gospel of Jesus Christ. Woody did just that as *Decision* magazine's first editor. Under Dr. Wirt's skillful care, close to five million copies of the magazine were distributed worldwide each month.

Woody had introduced me to rafting in 1983. What an exhilarating challenge and physical workout it turned out to be! He didn't introduce me to small ripples in the river; he baptized me into white-water rapids.

Woody was 72 years old on our first trip. He enjoyed every dip and turn in the river, even swimming in the water holes off the beaten path. Not content to stay in camp, Woody livened up the group by hiking up a creek to find a waterfall and beautiful pool below it to swim in—all the while giving a free lecture about the wonders of nature. The highlight of that trip was seeing Woody swan dive from a 15-foot-high ledge into the pool. (A feat, incidentally, that none of the younger bucks dared even to challenge). I like to call Woody "the world's oldest living boy."

Since that time, I have taken five wonderful rafting trips down the Tuolumne, Kalamath, and Snake Rivers. Each one presented its own unique challenges and beauty. Last year, Woody, now 85 years young in spirit, said to me in passing, "Mike, I would like to take one more river rafting trip with you."

Of course, my heart was both warmed and touched. This titan of masculinity was up for one more confrontation with nature and her demands. Quickly we put together a unique group of friends, ten couples in all, and chose the Tuolumne River once more. Our trip would take us through Yosemite National Park with its breathtakingly beautiful scenery.

The river has its own way of making a white-water rafting trip fun, fun, fun. The 1994-95 winter rains in California made headline news around the United States, and the snowpack was great. We expected the summer runoffs to give us a wonderful ride for two days and 18 miles of white water.

Yet we were worried that our vacation might be cut short because word was out from Colorado to California that several people had died and scores were injured while white-water rafting. The melting snow was causing some hairy rides through fast, turbulent rapids. The day we arrived, we were told that eight people had already perished on the lower part of the Tuolumne.

We heeded the warnings and promised to be especially careful to follow the directions of our experienced guides. Six weeks prior to our visit, the river had been so rough that it had been closed to rafters. Now the experts felt it was safe again. We were the first group to be allowed to raft since the river's closure and reopening.

The first day was a lot of fun, even though Woody and Ruth got dunked. Fortunately, they had been paired with Scott and Diana Holslag, the youngest couple on the trip. Scott is a 220-pound body builder and San Diego County sheriff, while Diana, a paralegal, keeps in great shape by working out three times a week in her family's San Diego fitness center. This handsome couple had been assigned to ride with the Wirts in case they needed extra care—not that Woody wanted any. It turned out that Scott and Diana joined the Wirts in a brief, frigid dip in the freshly melted, fast-moving water. Yet it was nothing dangerous.

The next day, after spending a peaceful night camping, we had breakfast, packed, and were soon ready to paddle the 200 feet to the head of Clavey Falls. Sandy and I were in the first raft, leading the charge. John and Marilyn Dahlberg were with us, paddling left, right, forward, and reverse as the guide shouted commands over the thunderous noise. "Yahoo," I yelled, "Yahoo," as the tremendous swell of water splashed our faces and drenched our bodies.

Since I was in the front, I could see that we had made it through without a hitch. But wait a minute—what was that wave building in front of us? We had dropped to the lowest point below the falls, yet this wave towered over us and was about to break over our boat. This was not supposed to happen. The next thing I knew, John and I were sputtering underwater in the most vicious rapids this 18-mile stretch of river had to throw at us.

It all happened so quickly. When I came up for air, I saw Marilyn and grabbed her arm, but the turbulence threw me under again into huge boulders on the bottom. That's when I realized my very survival was at stake. As I broke the surface again and gasped for air, I did my best to get onto my back in order to float downstream, as we had been taught in our safety lecture. It didn't work. For the third time some unseen force threw me under and I prayed, "Lord, don't let me die here." I had a great sense of peace, but I knew that death was hovering nearby.

Cold water has a tendency to zap you of your strength and any reserves you might have. No matter how good your physical condition might be, cold water can make you a weakling in a hurry. The cold kept me from getting air when I resurfaced. Instead, I took on another gallon or so of icy water. I thought it was just about over for me when I saw the next rapid approaching. Unable to fill my lungs with air, coughing up water, struggling to keep my head up above the current, I heard the shout of our oarsman. "Swim over here! Swim over here!" Although I am a decent swimmer, you couldn't call what I did "swimming." My arms simply had no strength; although I am a man who can bench press 200 pounds, I couldn't lift my arms out of the water. By dog-paddling, crawling, pulling myself along—whatever it took short of walking on the water—I was determined to make it to the rocks where the guide stood screaming for me.

When I finally made it, I realized I could not get out of the water or hold onto a rock. With the feeblest voice I have ever uttered, I cried, "Help me!" Thank God, the guide reached out a hand and pulled me up. I began coughing up water, emptying one full tummy. I knew I had just escaped death. Then it dawned on me—if I had had such a close call, what had happened to Sandy, John, and Marilyn? I immediately prayed for them. Just then the second raft over the falls capsized in the same spot we had. Ruth, Woody, Scott, Diana, and their guide all were thrown into the angry water.

My guide called the third boat over as it cleared the dangerous hole that had sucked down the first two groups. The people in the third boat were stunned when they popped over the ridge to begin their descent—stretched over half a mile, ten drenched people were grasping for safety among baggage, oars, supplies, rafts, and were bobbing downriver, now spinning, then disappearing.

It was 30 minutes before a boat could get upstream to pick me up and take me to safety. When I saw the raft coming, I could tell something was terribly wrong.

Dr. Fred Salley is one of the leading family physicians in San Diego. He and his lovely wife, Meliss, were on the beach tending the injured, along with Sheila Najor, Dr. Salley's head nurse. Apparently, Ruth Wirt had been swept violently under the current and had swallowed an enormous amount of water. When Doc Salley saw Ruth, he wasn't sure if she was alive or dead.

Woody, on the other hand, had been swept away so violently that he lost his shorts. He smashed into multiple rocks, badly cutting his knees and legs. The cold water stunned his 84-year-old body and took his breath away. The doc thought we might lose him. Burly Scott said that when he pulled Woody into a raft, he thought he was dead.

In counting heads, we realized some were still missing. Fortunately, the supply raft had followed the missing members of our group downstream, and picked them up. We linked up with them an hour later. When finally we took off for home, we found gear strewn five miles downriver. John and Marilyn both had suffered near-death experiences. As we got out of the rescue raft, Sandy had a hard time standing. After a thorough checkout by Dr. Salley and one of the guides (who was also an Emergency

Medical Technician), it was decided to splint Sandy's leg and consider the strong possibility that she had broken her thigh bone.

Hours later we finally made it to a country hospital—John with a swollen and sore wrist, Marilyn with a swollen ankle, me with minor scratches and bruises, and Sandy in her wet suit with driftwood tied to her leg as a splint. Fortunately, the X rays showed no break in the bone. Sandy had a deeply bruised leg, coupled by black and blue marks all over her lower body. She, too, had joined the club of "near-death experiences."

A week later as we all talked over what had happened, we were amazed to realize that none of us had been in the water for long. The cold temperature, the raging waters, the violent undertow, the heavy snowpack melting so quickly, had combined to cause the river to move swiftly, showing no mercy to anyone willing to challenge it. All of these factors added up to a harrowing experience for the 10 out of our 20 who went overboard. Yet God was faithful; we all made it out intact.

Finding Peace in Turmoil

As we travel the road of life, accidents are bound to join us somewhere along our journey. The right circumstances, the right factors, the right ingredients, the right people at the right time and in the right place could be a blessing . . . or could spell disaster.

What is it for you? The hurts you face today—are they like our rafting trip? You started out to have a good time, but it suddenly turned ugly. You meant for something good to happen, but things didn't go your way. It all happens so quickly, doesn't it?

When accidents intrude on our plans, it's crucial that we remember God is still on the throne. He is alive. He does care about the real-life situations we find ourselves in, the major disasters as well as the minor ones.

You may have had a triple tragedy or merely a fender bender. Nevertheless, you are still bleeding emotionally from it and are wondering if you will ever recover. God's Word insists that you can. Why not give the Lord a chance to work in your life to bring you healing?

Let me suggest that you pray about this right now. Give the Lord the opportunity to dress your hurts. Put the right cure into place for your life and let the healing begin.

> Dear heavenly Father, please help me to trust You in this process of dressing my hurt. Counsel me with Your Word, Lord, and speak to me through the Scriptures. Bind my heart with Your love and forgiveness. Take control of my situation and begin a healing process in me now, I ask. Father, I don't understand everything that You are going to do to cover my open pain and hurt; but I am going to trust You. In Jesus' name. Amen.

4

Fallout in the Family

The Tender Touch of God

Years ago I heard about a Swedish couple who were celebrating their fiftieth wedding anniversary. When the festivities ended, the woman turned to her husband and said,

> Sven, we've been miserable for 50 years. We've fought every day. We've disagreed on nearly everything, and I am convinced that we can't keep going like this. I have made a commitment to pray that God will help us solve this problem. I'm praying that He will take one of us home. And when He answers my prayer, I'm going to live with my sister in Gothenburg.

One day a family psychologist told me that just because a couple has been married 30 or 40 or even 50 years does not mean it must be a good marriage. At first his comment startled me, but then I began to understand his reasoning. Long years do not assure a happy marriage. Most of us have known of couples who say they are only staying together until the children are grown. Nowadays, even that kind of commitment is disappearing. In years past, marriage was synonymous with family. In today's fast-paced world, marriage seems equally synonymous with divorce.

Divorce in America

In 1976, slightly more than 2.1 million marriage licenses were issued in the United States—and almost 1.1 divorces were granted.[1] A ratio of 2 to 1! The U.S. Census Bureau gives the following figures:[2]

> In 1920, 1 divorce for every 7 marriages.
> In 1940, 1 divorce for every 6 marriages.
> In 1960, 1 divorce for every 4 marriages.
> In 1972, 1 divorce for every 3 marriages.

In 1991, Tampa, Florida, became the first place in America where you could get a divorce without leaving your car: Drive-thru divorces had become a reality.

Divorce is rampant in our society. I heard a statistic the other day that claimed only 35 percent of American children are living in a two-parent home.

Sadly, divorce has become so acceptable that, according to George Barna in his book *The Frog in the Kettle*, "By 2000, Americans will generally believe that a life spent with the same partner is both unusual and unnecessary."[3]

Assessing the Damage

As we near the end of the twentieth century, we now are able to assess the damage of the past 30 years to

American families. The fallout of divorce and remarriage is showing up everywhere. The toll is devastating. Read this letter to Ann Landers, along with her response:

Dear Ann Landers:

Ten years ago I left my wife and four teenagers to marry my secretary with whom I'd been having an affair. I felt I couldn't live without her. When my wife found out about us she went to pieces.

We were divorced. My wife went to work, and did a good job educating the boys. I gave her the house and part of my retirement fund.

I am fairly happy in my second marriage, but I'm beginning to see things in a different light. It hit me when I was a guest at our eldest son's wedding. That's all I was—a guest. I am no longer considered part of the family. My first wife knew everyone present, and they showered her with affection.

She remarried, and her husband has been taken inside the circle that was once ours. They gave the rehearsal dinner, and sat next to my sons and their sweethearts.

I was proud to have a young, pretty wife at my side. But it didn't make up for the pain when I realized that my children no longer love me. They treated me with courtesy, but there was no affection or real caring.

I miss my sons, especially around holiday time. I am going to try to build some bridges, but the prospects don't look very promising after being out of their lives for ten years. It is going to be difficult reentering now that they have a step-dad they like.

I'm writing in the hope that others will consider the ramifications before they jump. Just sign me

Second Thoughts in P.A.

Dear Second Thoughts:

I could use the rest of this column to reflect on "sowing and reaping," but it would serve no useful purpose.

I'm sure you also know that a father can't disappear for ten years and expect his sons to welcome him back with open arms. Sorry, Mister, your wife has earned their respect and devotion, and what's left over is going to the man who is now making their mother happy.[4]

This sad tale of pain and regret could be retold millions of times. Men and women look back on the decision they made to leave their families and judge it a mistake—but often it's too late. The pain and agony of divorce goes on and on. Especially for the children of divorce.

One study showed that children are more likely to suffer from depression when they grow up, if their parents divorce, than if one dies.

Our church operates a preschool, K-8, and high school. Members of our great staff often go beyond duties of the classroom and are drawn into difficult family situations. Up close, you see that the children of divorce go through deep, deep pain. One of our special education teachers helps those students who need just a little extra touch of Jesus, that tender touch of God which can help them learn a little easier.

Recently, a pastor shared the following letter from a learning-impaired student who is trusting his teacher with some heart-wrenching insights:

> Dear Mrs Carroll,
>
> My mom and Dad are geting Devarst. But i am still ok. I am trieing to get Beter. It is a hard to reakover from a Broken hart. So I am trieing to kep my head hie.
>
> Love, Layne

Real-life tragedies like these can break your heart. But the biggest tragedy is that we have forgotten what the prophet Malachi said so many centuries ago: "'For the LORD God of Israel says that *He hates divorce,* for it covers one's garment with violence,' Says the LORD of hosts. 'Therefore take heed to your spirit, that you do not deal treacherously'" (Malachi 2:16). Even in the church, we have ignored this scripture. And we have dismissed wise advice such as the following from James Dobson, who says we should not "permit the possibility of divorce to enter [our] thinking—divorce is no solution. It merely substitutes a new set of miseries for the ones left behind."[5]

Biblically speaking, divorce is undeniably wrong. God hates it. Yet being the weak, fallible humans that we are, we stumble into it at ever-increasing rates. Is there, then, anything to be done when we are faced with the searing pain of divorce? Is healing available?

Love Can Heal Anything

A salesman called his wife from a coin-operated phone in a distant city, finished the conversation, said good-bye, and hung up the receiver. As he was walking away, the phone rang. He went back and answered it, expecting to be informed of extra charges. But the operator said, "I thought you'd like to know. Just after you hung up, your wife said, 'I love you.'"

There's nothing like those three words, is there? "I love you." I figure that love can heal anything. So did the apostle Peter; that's why he wrote that "love will cover a multitude of sins" (1 Peter 4:8).

Love is the most powerful force on earth. It's not only the key to keeping a marriage alive, it's also the key to God healing our hurts. More of us should tap into the love of God—it's free, fulfilling, and available to all. It's that powerful love that can and does heal marriages. I know; it healed mine.

A Beach Bum Brain Surgeon?

Sandy and I met during Easter week, 1966. We were both 22 years old. It was at Sandy's twenty-second birthday party (to which I invited myself) that we really began to know each other.

She had graduated from the exclusive Stephens Girls College in Columbia, Missouri, and was finishing up her degree at Cal State Fullerton. Her father was president of a large, international corporation, and her mother was the daughter of a former North Dakota Secretary of Agriculture.

And me? I was a medical student at the University of Oregon Medical Center, finishing up my studies. I was going to be a brain surgeon. At least, that was my story.

In reality, I was a beach bum, out of work, surfing and tanning, going from beach party to beach party, living off of unemployment checks and the change I picked up from recycling soda-pop bottles.

Yet three weeks after Sandy's party, I found myself riding in a car with this sophisticated, well-educated, well-bred and well-mannered, long-legged blond beauty, on our way to Las Vegas where we got married. Unbelievable, you say. Exactly: That's just how I felt, too.

The members of Sandy's family were shocked by our sudden marriage, but were very generous to us. They bought us a house and gave us a car—all the amenities of middle-class America which I never had enjoyed. Yet this new lifestyle put an enormous amount of pressure on my "free spirit," and I soon began to go astray. Hardly a day went by when I wasn't either drunk, stoned or otherwise miserable.

Eventually, Sandy got fed up with me. She knew that I was nuts and judged it best to back out of a bad situation. She loved me dearly and always wanted to "fix" me, but she finally gave up. It had become clear that I

70

carried too much baggage from my childhood and too much guilt from my teens to be redeemed. We already had one child, Mindi (who is as breathtakingly beautiful today as she was as a little girl), and Sandy was pregnant with our second child. But before David was born, Sandy—for her own sake and the future of our children—divorced me. She had every reason in the world to do so. I was immature, an emotional basket case, unable to accept responsibility, and lost.

But sometime later something totally unexpected happened. I met Jesus Christ. With Jesus in my heart, God cured me of the ugliness of my sin and gave me a second chance at life.

When Sandy saw the change that came over me, she knew something was different—she just didn't know what. Her ex-husband, Michael, seemed to be a new man. *Something* had happened to him. What was it?

Because I wanted Sandy to understand the "new me," I invited her to attend a baptismal service in the Pacific Ocean, officiated by Pastor Chuck Smith. Pastor Chuck was baptizing 2000 people that night at Pirate's Cove in Corona Del Mar. As he spoke, Sandy felt the conviction of her sin and gave her heart to Jesus. That night she was born again and baptized, and her life began to change as drastically as had mine. Both of us began to attend the Bible studies which Pastor Chuck led at church. Our lives were transformed as we listened to the Word on Sunday mornings, Sunday nights, Monday nights, and Thursday nights.

Finally, after almost three years of divorce, God graciously reunited us in marriage. God truly is the Healer!

Our marriage continues to grow after all of these years. We were blessed with Mindi, David, Megan, Jonathan, and Phillip. Each one of them has been a special joy to us. We love each of them for their own individuality and the special person that they are. We can't thank God enough for healing our broken marriage and giving us a second chance.

I love the words of King Solomon in Psalm 128 (KJV): "Blessed is every one that feareth the LORD; that walketh in his ways. For thou shalt eat the labour of thine hands: happy shalt thou be, and it shall be well with thee. Thy wife shall be as a fruitful vine by the sides of thine house: thy children like olive plants round about thy table. Behold, that thus shall the man be blessed that feareth the LORD." How correct Solomon was concerning my family!

Too Much for You, Not for Him

Yes, God knows how to heal our hurts. If your own hurts include a bad family situation or marriage, then let God heal you. Unlike us, He does such a great job at it. The problems you may be facing in your marriage are too much for you to handle. But for the Lord, they are easy.

Possibly today, you are right in the middle of a miserable time in your marriage. You may even question if you married the right person. You wonder, *Will this marriage work out?*

When Ronald Reagan ran for the office of president of the United States of America, he chose George Bush to be his running mate. George's wife, Barbara Bush, said she was told that because both she and her husband are Geminis, "We probably should never have gotten married." She paused, then said with a twinkle in her eye that she didn't "know what to do about it now after 43 years."

It may be difficult for you to try to go even another year, but give Jesus a chance. He performed His very first miracle at a wedding feast. He can still perform a miracle for you. Marriage in itself is a miracle.

Jesus once told His disciples that with faith the size of a grain of mustard seed, they could move mountains. It might be years since you exercised faith, but today would be a great time to put faith to work and trust God to change your marriage. Let God's tender touch stop the bleeding between you and your spouse.

Or perhaps you're not having marriage troubles; your marriage already has crumbled. If you are hurting terribly from an ugly divorce, God can bring His healing touch even there—if you will let Him. Is your pain caused by the divorce of your parents when you were still very young? If so, please take it from me: The tender touch of God can heal your hurt, too.

No matter what has happened in your marriage or family, you can find tremendous hope in God. He can bring your lives to His cross and make you into new people. Sandy and I are living proof that God can put together that which man destroys. You may be like the man who wrote to Ann Landers, full of regrets and guilt. But know this, my friend: The tender touch of God can stop even this bleeding in your life. There is no hurt so big that it is beyond His healing touch. Not even the deep hurts inflicted on children by abuse or neglect.

Children of Abusive Homes

As president of Youth Development International (YDI), I am always concerned for children. YDI operates the National Youth Crisis Hotline, 1-800-Hit Home. In 1995 we logged about 400,000 calls from kids age 18 and under.

These kids tell us that the American home is sick. Many of these children have been severely abused. We know that if these victims are not helped, it is likely that a horrible cycle of pain and hurt will continue. Some studies say as many as 70 percent of abusive parents were themselves abused as children. According to the Children's Defense Fund, *every 24 hours* in the United States:

- 437 teens are arrested for drunk driving
- 1206 unwed teens have abortions
- 1365 unwed teens give birth
- 1512 teens drop out of school
- 3288 teens run away from home
- 135,000 teens carry guns to school[6]

The ramifications of these hurts to the next generation are staggering. If our government was smart, it would realize that we won't go broke as a nation because we have no money today; our nation will go broke tomorrow, because our children are bankrupt—morally, financially, and relationally. They have never been taught the value of patriotism or the importance of human life. *It must be okay to kill another kid on the street*, they think, *since it is okay to kill an unborn baby in the womb.*

Our kids bear the brunt of the devastation caused by family breakups. But even in the healthiest of families, kids can make mistakes and get hurt. I personally know this kind of pain, too.

Falling off the Fence

Do you remember the old children's rhyme from Mother Goose that went like this:

> Humpty Dumpty sat on the Wall
> Humpty Dumpty had a great Fall
> All the kings horses
> And all the kings men
> Couldn't put Humpty
> Back together again.

I'm grateful that all of our children have the grace, elegance, poise, and composure of Sandy. Unfortunately, they also picked up some of my impatience, frenetic mind, and borderline humor. None of our kids is more like me than our beautiful daughter Megan. Sandy calls this story "Falling off the Fence"; I call it "Thank God." Megan calls it a miracle—a classic example of how pain can be used to change our lives and draw us closer to God.

Megan is Miss Congeniality. When she was little, you might have thought she was Shirley Temple's replacement. When *Annie* became a hit movie, Megan got a red dress and a red wig, just like Annie, and wandered through the house, singing at the top of her lungs, "Tomorrow, tomorrow, I luv ya, tomorrow." I think she wore the wig to school five days straight, along with the bright-red dress and a white belt around her tiny waist.

One day I surprised her. I told Megan that a surprise friend was waiting for her upstairs in the game room. She had no idea who'd she find there, but she was excited to find out. After a few moments, there was a loud shout and I knew they had met.

The friend, however, was not flesh and blood. She was a five-foot, tall cardboard cutout of Annie from the video store that I picked up for 20 dollars. For a second or two, Megan actually thought the real Annie was there. She's always been a live wire with the energy of three or four kids her age.

Megan has been blessed with beauty, talent, charm, and wit. But like most of us, she has discovered that personal strengths can become great weaknesses.

Megan strayed from the Lord during her teen years. The first major fall came when she was 18 and attending college in Nashville. I'll never forget how I heard the news.

I was flying to Toronto to join Larry Backlund and the Billy Graham School of Evangelism team. I flew myself there because I had several speaking engagements along the way. I called Sandy from the terminal at a small Michigan airport while the plane was being refueled. She asked, "Are you sitting or are you standing?"

"I'm standing," I said.

"You'd better sit down," she instructed me.

"Did someone die in our family?"

"No, but you'd better sit down."

"Hey, you know there's nothing that can knock me over. I've heard it all before. What's up?"

"Megan got married!"

The wind went out of me. I fell against the wall so loudly that the only passenger in the commuter terminal turned around to see what the clamor was about. I looked at him and said, "My little girl eloped." Sandy began to talk again, but I couldn't handle it. I said, "I can't talk right now. I'll call you later." Five minutes later I called back and said, "Did I just call you and you said Megan got married?" When she confirmed this was true, I said, "Bear with me, I'll call you from the hotel room tonight."

I was a wreck when I got up to speak at my first session in Toronto. I told the audience that my little baby, my little Annie, had run away and gotten married to a friend in college. When the session was over, a woman came up to me—the wife of one of the ministers—threw her arms around me, and gave me the world's biggest hug. She said, "This is a hug from your wife who couldn't be here with you at this time." Her husband looked at me and said, "Mike, everything will turn out just fine. Our daughter did the same thing. You'll survive, and so will she."

But everything didn't turn out just fine. The marriage was a disaster, and two years later Megan and her husband were divorced.

Sandy and I have prayed for Megan every day that she would be happy and at peace with herself and with Jesus. After she returned to San Diego, Megan's job transferred her away from us to Scottsdale, Arizona. She was maturing as a woman in her new managerial position, and the men in the singles scene found her very attractive. The freedom she found being on her own in an upwardly mobile desert town enchanted her. She made friends quickly, as usual—and also began living in the fast lane.

One night she went to a party with a friend and had too much to drink. A friend whom she trusted and loved tried to carry her into the house, but since he too had been drinking, it was a bad idea. He accidentally dropped Megan, and the fall literally smashed her face.

She was unconscious when the paramedics arrived. The impact knocked out a front tooth, broke her nose, and inflicted the mother of all bruises on her face. It wasn't a pretty sight.

When Megan woke up in the emergency room of a local hospital, she wasn't sure where she was. The doctor used smelling salts to awaken her. They had been wiring the top of her mouth together, trying desperately to save her front tooth.

Her boyfriend had called his parents to come and help him get through this ugly night. He had been raised in a very strong Christian family, with grandparents who served as missionaries to India and a father who was deeply involved in Christian ministry. The first face she recognized belonged to her boyfriend's mother. Her first words were a question: "Do you hate me?" Megan was more concerned about what others thought about her than her own condition. These wonderful people lovingly took Megan into their home and spent many hours helping her recuperate.

In response to many tears and prayers, God started doing a fresh, new work in my daughter. Megan and her boyfriend, both raised with the knowledge of God, had been living worldly lives, trying to find other ways and means to gain happiness. In their own words, "God used the physical and emotional pain of the incident to wake us up and get us off the fence."

These two prodigals have learned a tremendous, life-long lesson. Their pain was a wake-up call to get off the fence and get right with God. They knew that God used this tragic event as if He had pushed them off the fence to bring them closer to the Lord, closer to their families, and closer to each other.

Humpty-Dumpty may not have been able to be put back together again by all the king's horses and all the king's men, but the Lord was able to put back together Megan and her boyfriend.

Remember that Scripture from Hosea 6 we looked at earlier? He has torn, He has smitten, but He will heal and He will bind up. I think my daughter's story fits that verse. God was using something painful to bring about something good. Megan and her boyfriend both made a commitment to stop drinking, to spend more time in Christian environments, to change their lifestyles, and to glorify God with their actions.

The Time Is Now

My friend, whatever pain you may be enduring from a difficult marriage, an ugly divorce, a prodigal child, or some other family trauma, God wants to bring healing to you. Perhaps the pain is many years old, and you grew up confused and brokenhearted and never found healing for this deep hurt. Whatever the pain and whenever it occurred, you can pray right this moment and ask Jesus Christ to begin binding up the hurt and pain in your life.

You can choose to live in your past and be miserable, or you can reach out to God and be healed. You can pray right this minute that God would help you.

> Dear God, please touch my heart and heal it from the pain. My family situation is one that desperately needs You. Come this very day, dear Holy Spirit, and fill me with hope. I reach out to You, Jesus, and ask that You will forgive my anger and bitterness. Give me love for those people whom I once loved. Please, heavenly Father, hear my prayer to You today and work on behalf of our family. In Jesus' name, Amen.

God is the great Healer. And He wants to bring you His tender touch today. So why not let Him?

5

The Mr. Dillon
Syndrome

—*The Tender Touch of God*—

T he world is full of people who don't want to get better. They don't want to be healed or made well. They get their identity and sometimes their self-worth from their hurt. I call it the "Mr. Dillon Syndrome."

One of television's first programs was also my favorite during my growing-up years. I loved "Gunsmoke." Each week Sheriff Matt Dillon (played by James Arness) would work out all the problems of his town. Dennis Weaver played Sheriff Dillon's sidekick, Chester. His character had a bad leg and couldn't run or walk without dragging that leg behind him.

Invariably, each show featured at least one scene where Chester would come shuffling to the saloon where Miss Kitty usually was talking with the sheriff. This is where my favorite line normally appeared. "Mr. Dillon! Mr. Dillon," he would shout, dragging his crippled leg behind.

As long as Chester was part of the series, he never did get that crippled leg taken care of. He was still crying "Mr. Dillon!" when the sun set in the west for the last time.

Mr. Dillon Lives On

Chester and "Gunsmoke" have long since disappeared from the nation's prime-time airwaves, but there are thousands, perhaps millions of people who still like to be recognized by their "bad leg" (whatever it might be). You can see them hobbling down the thoroughfares of life and shouting, "Mr. Dillon! Mr. Dillon!"

When I counsel people who struggle with the same problems that the Lord has given me victory over, I see a tendency for them not to believe they can get better. They think it is a lot safer to just go on living with this crippling hurt than to let it go and be healed. It reminds me of a folk story in the Ozark Mountains of Arkansas that goes like this:

A man went to visit a neighbor who he found rocking on his front porch. As the two men conversed, they were disturbed by the homeowner's dog, who continually moaned and groaned. Finally, the visitor asked, "What is wrong with your dog?" "Well," the man answered, "the poor ole dog is trying to sleep, but he is lying on a nail. He hurts enough that he can't sleep, but he doesn't hurt enough to make him get up and move."

So often we are just like that old dog. We moan and groan about our marriages, our diets, our jobs, etc., but we don't seem to hurt enough to get serious about doing something about improving our situation. Our continuing

pain is the fruit of refusing to take immediate act
stop the bleeding.

The Great Cover-up

One of the most common ways we fail to address our
hurts is by trying to cover them up. In so doing, we unwittingly follow the pattern set by Adam and Eve in the
Garden of Eden. When Adam and Eve sinned against
God, immediately they covered their nakedness with fig
leaves. Then they hid from Him. When God came looking for them and cried out, "Adam, where are you?"
Adam and Eve appeared before Him to confess they had
disobeyed His word and had covered their nakedness.

I suppose Adam and Eve blended in quite well with
their environment, camouflaged as they were by fig
leaves. Yet their cover-up did nothing to heal their pain;
it only made it worse.

How this paints a picture of the ways we often try to
cover up our hurts instead of dealing with them! Yet covering up the hurt does nothing to bring healing. We must
stop the bleeding and bind up the wound; otherwise, we
will lose the joy of living—or even life itself.

I think of Vince Foster, lifetime friend of President Bill
Clinton. One article said their friendship could be traced
to their kindergarten days. Foster had been given a very
powerful position as special counsel to the president of
the United States of America. Yet one day he was found
dead, the apparent victim of suicide.

No clear picture exists why Vince Foster committed
suicide. Some people believe he knew of underhanded
dealings that took place while Mr. Clinton was governor
of Arkansas, but the truth behind his suicide appears to
have gone to the grave with him.

What could have been so terrible in Foster's life that
death became a better answer than life? Could some

"sacred cows" have raised their heads? Did his problems seem invincible? How tragic it is when people lose sight of the Bible's view of living.

If we choose to cover up our hurts and not address them, very soon we will be wondering why we are living such shallow lives. We become like the Shakespearean actors who wore a mask of laughter over their faces to cover the frowns that expressed their real feelings.

Searching in All the Wrong Places

Covering up our hurt isn't the only way to lose the joy of living. An equally effective way to warp our personality is to seek hard after happiness, without ever seeking the Creator of happiness. Do you remember the simple California longshoreman Eric Hoffer? His was a simple, down-to-earth form of philosophy. One of his quotes rings so true for so many: "The search for happiness is one of the chief sources of unhappiness."[1]

Madonna sang of her "material girl." Robert Tilton preached his "$1,000 seed faith" message. Many television salesmen are hawking their videos and cassette tapes, promising us a new body, flat stomach, scratchless wax jobs for our cars, faster reading skills, a bigger vocabulary, the ability to learn a new language in 30 days—and if you can't manage that, then buy the music of the "oldies but goodies" to bring back those golden memories of yesteryear.

Those of us with a hair loss problem can find it taken care of on television. We are promised we will find happiness by having more hair, guaranteed. All we have to do is get a can of special hair spray and paint our head. Voilà! There we have it. We'll look 10 to 20 years younger and really be happy.

Can you imagine that? How gullible we have become! Real business people put up thousands of dollars for television production and viewing time to tell balding people, "Happiness is in a can." So we order on the toll-free 800 line and give the telemarketer our credit-card number and wait four to six weeks for the arrival of our new article of happiness. When it finally comes, often we have forgotten that we even ordered it. The quality is shabby and we threaten to return it, but we don't. We say to ourselves, "What's the use? I am too busy, and it will be too much of a hassle anyway." Our garages are filled with "happiness gadgets." We are the first generation that has so many material goods, gadgets, toys, and the like that we have allowed an entire industry to grow up around our impulse purchases.

We have so much excess (and most of it on credit) that our closets cannot handle it. So we move it into the garage. Our garage becomes so cluttered that we then go to the self-storage units to pay someone not only to store it, but also to secure it under lock and key, with razor wire on top of the fences. The storage business has really boomed since the baby boomers blossomed. It looks pretty much like they named it well, doesn't it? "*Self*-storage."

The Beatles sang, "Yesterday—all my troubles seemed so far away. Now it looks as if they're here to stay; O, I believe in yesterday." Eric Hoffer said it well, didn't he? "The search for happiness is one of the chief sources of unhappiness." Just ask O.J. Simpson.

This former NFL great rode his athletic prowess to tremendous success, both on the field and off. But though he looked happy and content, listen carefully to these words that appeared in an interview in the June 12, 1978, edition of *People* magazine. This was 16 years *before* the District Attorney of Los Angeles arrested O.J. for the murder of his second wife, Nicole Brown Simpson, and her friend, Ron Goldman:

> I sit in my house in Buffalo and sometimes I get
> so lonely it's unbelievable. Life has been so good
> to me. I've got a great wife, good kids, money, my
> own health—and I'm lonely and bored. . . . I often
> wondered why so many rich people commit sui-
> cide. Money sure isn't a cure-all.[2]

I think of the words spoken to me by a masseur who
was attending to my bad back. "It's sad the prisons
which people build for themselves," he told me. "They
stuff their pain in the tension of their necks. Or maybe
the strain in their backs. They choose to live in these
self-made prisons instead of confronting the pain."

Don't you be one of them. Don't opt for the Mr. Dillon Syndrome. Face your problems squarely. And the
first way to begin doing that is by assessing the damage.

Assess the Damage

In my capacity as a chaplain with various San Diego
law-enforcement units, I often ride along with officers on
patrol. When I have been on the scene of an accident or a
shooting, I've noticed that the paramedic team will first
assess the damage. It is from this assessment that these
talented people begin the process to "stop the bleeding"
and bind up the wounds so the injured person can be
transported to the hospital.

In the same way, one of the first things we need to
do to address our own hurts is to assess the situation. I
wonder: Have you ever really assessed your situation?
Maybe it's time you sat back for a while and let the things
surface that are hurting you. Take the time to evaluate
and assess your situation. Think of it as a time for damage control, a time to stop the bleeding.

Don't lose the joy of living! There is hope, and you
are going to be better.

I read of a pastor who, during the Sunday worship service, came to the time when everyone greets one another. He said, "Psychologists tell us that one out of three people in America is in need of therapy. This morning, shake hands with two people. If they seem okay, you're it."

I find that if my problems warp my personality, then my thinking is askew. Usually, I think it's the other two who aren't okay. But when I begin to work on my problems, I stop looking at others through fun-zone mirrors. I see them just as they are, in reality. I find I'm the one who's distorted!

Henry Van Dyke wrote a poem to encourage his readers to go forward. It takes courage to look at a bad wound. It also takes courage for the wounded to try to stop the bleeding. Listen to the words of the poet:

> The mountains that inclose the vale
> With walls of granite, steep and high,
> Invite the fearless foot to scale
> Their stairway toward the sky.
> The restless, deep, dividing sea
> That flows and foams from shore to shore,
> Calls to its sunburned chivalry,
> "Push out, set sail, explore!"
>
> The bars of life at which we fret,
> That seem to prison and control,
> Are but the doors of daring, set
> Ajar before the soul.
>
> Say not, "Too poor," but freely give;
> Sigh not, "Too weak," but boldly try;
> You never can begin to live
> Until you dare to die.[3]

Jesus put it this way: "Whosoever shall seek to save his life shall lose it; and whosoever shall lose his life shall preserve it" (Luke 17:33 KJV).

It is possible that you are looking deeply into your heart right now, and the Holy Spirit has shown you the hurt from a past era of your life. You don't need to continue to bleed from this wound. God wants to heal you—but first you must fully recognize the hurt for what it is.

Take the Right Action

Still, recognizing our hurt, as crucial as that is, isn't enough. We must *take action*. If we don't take action, this hurt can warp our personality and our perspective of living, just as surely as looking in a fun-zone mirror can. If we remain inert, we will see through the eyes of distortion. Lack of action can leave permanent scars.

So what kind of action should we take? Most people respond to hurts in various ways—not all of them the best for their own good. If we address our pain in adverse ways, hurts will likely begin following us—and often they soon quit following and begin to lead. The list goes on and on of the tragic lives that have gone down to the grave without any joy or happiness.

Don't let the past or the trauma of the past keep you from heading into the future. You may feel as if you would be unfaithful to the memory of a dear one if you take action. You may think that life is not worth living because of your difficult situation, so you stagnate in time. Oh sure, you pay your bills, go to church, wave at your neighbors—but as one man told me, "Mike, my life is sad. Just remember every time you see me playing golf or at church, I may look happy; but inside, I am miserable."

My friend, don't let these hurts become sacred cows to you. I heard the story of a minister who had just hired a new secretary. Formerly, she was employed at the Pentagon. Upon reorganizing her new boss' filing system, she labeled one drawer "Sacred" and the other "Top Sacred."

Let's open those drawers and courageously face what's inside.

If today you realize that your identity is in your weakness, the first step toward healing is to admit that you have the Mr. Dillon Syndrome. You can't imagine what it would be like if you weren't "the invalid," "poor old mom," "druggie Harold," or some other character in the parade of life.

These false images sometimes block us from the real point of living. So often we lose the joy of living because we don't give immediate attention to that which is hurting us. But if we want to feel the warmth of the sunshine on our faces once more, we must take action, however uncomfortable it may be.

Good-bye, Mr. Dillon

Do you remember during the 1960s how a whole generation tried to disguise itself? There were long, fuzzy beards, rose-colored granny glasses, hip huggers, bell-bottoms, peace symbols, thongs, Neru jackets, long hair, paisley-painted Volkswagens, gurus, mantras, marijuana, LSD, and love-ins. Conservative families had spent years raising conservative kids, then, BOOM! An explosion ripped apart the facade of the sixties, revealing some pretty rotten fruit.

Often we take our problems and dress them up with cute flower patterns and dazzling beads. We try to adopt some identity that will draw outsiders away from the real us, in hopes that we will be more acceptable. Tragically, we often fool not only others, but ourselves, too.

My friend, you cannot afford to live this type of life. Give up your false identity as someone mentally crippled by an ugly situation from the past. Abandon your false identity as the ex-alcoholic, ex-drug addict, ex-pornography addict. It seems that everywhere we turn these days there is some program that promises to help us slog through life with some false identity.

I've seen so many hurting people trying so hard to "get through" that they never arrive. There are many "step" programs that outline 10 or 12 or 15 certain steps one must take to find peace. There are many well-intentioned people directing well-intentioned programs designed to help you face yourself, to draw you out from behind your disguise, to get that bum leg of yours healed. Yet most fall short by not telling the simple truth: Someone already has done everything that needs to be done to stop your bleeding. And He will stop your bleeding if you will just let Him.

I ask you to take just one step into God's program: Step toward the cross of Christ. You can do that by approaching His throne in prayer. Lay your burden at His feet. The Bible says, "Casting all your care upon Him, for He cares for you" (1 Peter 5:7). It may be difficult for you to humble yourself and cast your cares upon Him—you may be a self-made person who has always handled everything yourself. You've never turned to anyone for help, especially the Lord. To go to the Lord now may make you feel like a hypocrite. You may be asking, "Why would God help me now when I have ignored Him all of these years?" It's very simple. *Because He loves you!*

You may reply, "Yes, Mike, but what if He rejects me?" Trust me, He won't. It was Jesus Himself who said, "Come to Me, all you who labor and are heavy laden, and I will give you rest. Take My yoke upon you and learn from Me, for I am gentle and lowly in heart, and you will find rest for your souls. For My yoke is easy and My burden is light" (Matthew 11:28-30).

This is where you can begin. Now! Today! Learn of Jesus, and you will see that He "stopped the bleeding" for everyone who came to Him for help. The four Gospels in the New Testament paint a picture of Someone who gave

His very life for us so that we might live. More than anyone in the universe, He wants you to bid adieu to Mr. Dillon.

To help you say your good-byes, perhaps you could repeat the following prayer right now. There's nothing magical in the words, but the One who hears is longing for you to reach out to Him today through them (or something like them). Take a moment now to pray this simple prayer, just before we move on to the second part of this book:

> Dear Lord, may Your Holy Spirit come to me right now and open my eyes. May I see that I do not need to go on limping through life with the great problems and hurts that beset me. Show me that I do not need to limp from week to week, as Chester did on Gunsmoke. Give me the courage to drop my disguises and the false identities which I hide behind. I ask for Your help today. And Father, please give it to me in Jesus' name. Amen.

PART TWO
Dress the Wound

The Tender Touch of God

6

Our Part, God's Part

---The Tender Touch of God---

Remember the "divine healing regimen" I outlined in the introduction? Here it is again:

Stop the Bleeding
Dress the Wound
Let God Heal

There is a difference between stopping the bleeding and dressing the wound. In the first part of this book, we talked about identifying the hurt that is causing us so much pain. We learned to call on God to "stop the bleeding" and said that if we don't take immediate action to stop the bleeding, we lose the joy of living. Our personality gets warped—in extreme cases like the employee who shoots the boss.

95

We also discovered that if we don't stop the bleeding, we may wind up with a permanent, ugly scar. We can get a chip on our shoulder or become bitter in our outlook at life; long-held grudges build up. So we recognized that stopping the bleeding is an immediate necessity.

Yet that is only the first part of God's healing regimen. The second is "Dress the Wound." That's what we want to investigate in this second part of *The Tender Touch of God*. What is our part in the healing process? What does God ask us to do? What steps must we take to get beyond the pain and hurt and take hold once more of the abundant life?

Pushing in the Glass

When Sandy was pregnant with our fourth child, Megan, one of Sandy's best friends, Betsy Johnson (the wife of the 1960 Olympic gold medalist Rafer Johnson and godmother of our son David), had organized a baby shower for Sandy. Though Betsy and Rafer lived in the Los Angeles area, Betsy's mother and father owned a beautiful ranch in the North County of San Diego. That's where it was decided to hold the shower.

On the day of the shower we happily greeted all the invited guests. At the appointed hour, all of the guests had arrived except for one other couple and their children. After waiting quite some time, we decided to begin without them.

Not long after we began opening presents and enjoying the sight of all our children playing together in the swimming pool, the phone rang. The call was for me. As I excused myself, I wondered who in the world would know I was here.

I soon had my answer: It was a California highway patrolman. He informed me that the family we were expecting had been in a bad automobile accident about ten miles from the ranch. The officer asked me to come to the scene of the accident immediately. As I drove to the scene, my mind was churning with questions. What possibly could have happened? Why didn't my friend Dick call me himself?

Upon arrival, I identified myself and an officer told me that Dick, his wife, Carol, and their three children were all in ambulances on the way to the emergency center at Palomar Hospital. He gave me directions to the hospital and told me I would be only 15 minutes behind them. As I returned to my car, I noticed a man lying on the side of the highway, receiving medical attention from the paramedics.

I discovered this was the driver of the car that caused the collision. Apparently, he had tried to cross the four-lane highway without looking both ways and was broadsided at 50 MPH by Dick's van.

I was able to pray with the badly injured man, along with a patrolman standing nearby who identified himself as a Christian. When we were finished, I headed out to find my friends, hoping that all of them were still alive.

At the emergency room I spoke with nurses who gave me a quick evaluation of the family's injuries. Carol was in the worst condition, so she was rushed into the care of specialists. I was allowed to visit the various emergency and trauma rooms and pray for Dick and his children. Dick gave me the story as best he could recollect it.

The impact of the collision literally bent the other man's car in half and threw Carol out the van's front windshield. Dick was pinned in the van behind the steering wheel, while his three kids sitting in the camper area of the van were thrown about the interior of the vehicle. As Carol lay on the pavement, the van swung toward her and miraculously stopped just inches from her head. There is little doubt her head would have been crushed had the van failed to stop where it did. God had intervened.

Before the police and rescue workers arrived, Dick managed to free himself and climb out through the smashed windshield. Staggering to the back of the van, he found his wife lying in a pool of blood, her shattered face filled with glass slivers. Dick thought she looked almost dead—unconscious, unable to talk, but obviously in critical condition. Immediately, he thought to lay his hands upon her neck and pray that God would work a miracle. That done, he began to help his children out of the van as the rescue team arrived.

Although no one knew it at the time, Carol should have bled to death. The windshield glass had severed a major artery in her neck. Because of all the blood, Dick was unable to see that a thick piece of glass had punctured the side of Carol's bleeding neck. When Dick laid his hands upon her neck, he actually pushed the glass further in. This act was credited with saving her life; Dick unwittingly had stopped the bleeding. Otherwise, she would most likely have bled to death before being transported to the hospital. Dick had stopped the bleeding; now it was the doctors' turn to dress the wound.

That is the same place we have reached in this book. Once we have identified our problem and have stopped the bleeding, it is necessary to move to the next step of the healing process: dressing the wound. Above all, the wound must be dressed correctly so infection doesn't set in.

The dressing of Carol's wound took months to complete. Because her face was full of splintered windshield glass, the plastic surgeons had to work painstakingly at the damage. Every few weeks, Carol had to return to the doctor's office and have more glass removed, along with more scrubbing of the wounds and cleaning of her face. Each time she was covered with fresh bandages. Carol's healing was completed in sections as various parts of her face were dressed and bandaged. Finally, this young, vibrant mother was put back together again.

You know, often we think all we have to do is throw a bandage on our wounds and they will be okay in a couple of days. But Carol's accident illustrates that dressing serious wounds can take a long time—sometimes months, even years. But if the procedure is done correctly, true healing is the result.

Stop the Infection

When doctors dress a wound, they apply medicines that stop the spread of germs. They apply a healing lotion to counteract infection and enhance the healing process.

Physicians dress a wound in different ways, depending upon the nature of the injury. A burn victim receives a different type of dressing than does someone who broke his arm. Gunshot wounds and stabbing wounds penetrate the body in different ways and so need to be dressed differently. Some people get a tetanus shot as part of the physician's curative plan, while others do not.

Just as it is important for us to keep ourselves free of infection from wounds to the body, so is it imperative that we keep ourselves free of "infection" from wounds to the soul. As disease attacks the body, in the same manner sin attacks the soul. If it goes unchecked, the damage can be disastrous. If our wound is caused by sin and we don't deal with it, the "infection" can grow far worse than the original wound.

For example, consider someone who steals from his employer. After an investigation, management identifies the thief and has him arrested. The court finds the thief guilty, fines him 10,000 dollars, and sentences him to one year in jail. A lot of hurt is inflicted on the man's family while he sits in jail. Even once he is released, the pain continues; now he has the responsibility to pay the fine which the court levied. Ten thousand dollars taken out of the family's budget over a two-year period puts a strain on the family. Now the pain and hurt of stealing, being caught, judged, and sentenced is turning into additional suffering (an "infection").

The marriage now faces a tension that didn't exist two years ago. The wife feels betrayed, disappointed, and used. Bickering and fighting become frequent, eventually leading to physical abuse—which the children see. The kids now become rebellious because of what they see going on between Mom and Dad. They start skipping school and getting into trouble on campus, their grades slip, and their attitudes plummet.

Before long, the suffering turns into an open, festering wound, far worse than the original injury. Divorce papers are filed, a court date is set, and soon another family unit is torn apart.

How could such a disaster have been prevented? To dress such a wound as this, it would be necessary for all the parties involved to seek help. Only after facing the nature of the hurt and examining its cause can it be dealt with. It will not get better on its own. The idea that "time heals everything" simply isn't true. While many wounds require significant amounts of time to properly heal, they won't heal all by themselves. We must take a hands-on approach to recovering our health.

I don't know what kind of healing regimen is required in your case. You may come from a family with a history of alcohol abuse; in fact, that may be your own problem. Listen: Your wound is not going to heal with alcohol. Some people think the bleeding can be stopped with alcohol, but it can't. I know—I tried, and it doesn't work. In fact, abuse of alcohol shows that you are still bleeding. Many a beautiful home has been destroyed because of alcohol. Wonderful husbands and wives, good fathers and mothers weep tonight because the glory of their home and family has been shattered—never to be again—simply because of booze.

Or maybe that's not your wound at all. Maybe your wound was caused by a death in the family, a fractured relationship, the loss of a job, sexual abuse, or a personal failure. It doesn't matter what it is—the wound has to be dressed. And it has to be dressed in the right way.

Scores of self-help organizations and 30-minute videos are available which guarantee you a cure for whatever troubles you. Some of them really will help you crawl along in life. They'll give you tips on how to drag your crippled soul from one part of the dump to another. But their programs will not cure you. In some cases, the only real cure available is a miracle. But I have good news for you! God has warehouses full of miracles, in all shapes, sizes, and colors. He has one just for you. The real cure, the only certain cure, is to cry out to the Lord for help. Let Him give you the hope that you need; that is the cure. Yet you, too, have a part to play in your own healing. It may not be easy and it may not be fun, but it's the only way to lay hold of the healing you so desperately need.

Sometimes There's Pain

It isn't always true, but sometimes dressing a wound can be a painful process. Our oldest son, David, fell from his bicycle when he was seven years old. He badly scraped his arm on the road, embedding small chunks of gravel in the wound. When we arrived at the emergency room, the doctor checked for broken bones and then had the nurse cleanse and dress the wound. It was a difficult process for a seven-year-old.

The nurse poured antiseptic on David's open wound and abrasions. Of course, my son let his displeasure be known. Then came the really painful part of the process: The nurse took a scrub brush and scrubbed the wound thoroughly. David and I had to negotiate to get through that part of the procedure. I told him that if the nurse didn't scrub the wound, she would not be able to remove all of the unseen pieces of gravel. If she were to dress the wound without properly preparing it, infection could flare up underneath the dressing and in a few days cause a far worse situation than the original one.

David simply had to "bite the bullet" and let the nurse proceed. It wasn't pleasant, but it was necessary. No infection resulted, and David was soon back on his bike, tearing around the neighborhood as if nothing had ever happened.

Dressing the wounds of our soul can be even more painful than dressing physical wounds. But we can't let that stop us. We can't risk infection and bigger problems down the road.

I wonder, do you need simply to "bite the bullet" and persevere until your wound is properly dressed? I won't promise that dressing your wound will be pleasant or without pain. But I will promise that if you do your part now, God will be free to bring glorious, wonderful, powerful, divine healing to your soul. And isn't that what you really want?

Now Is the Time

Today would be a great day for you to reach out to Jesus. Ask Him to dress your wound and make you whole. Why not pray right now and ask the Lord to take any pride or prejudice out of your heart that might be holding back the dressing of your hurt and pain? Ask the Lord to remove any excuses or resistance which you may be putting forward. Finally, ask God to bind up the hurt in your life and begin a healing process. You can speak any words that you wish while addressing your heavenly Father; He promises to hear every sincere word.

Speak truth from your heart, and you will find a great release. Use the following prayer as an example to help you communicate with the One who loves you the most. The One who wants to help you the most. Open the door to your heart and let the Lord do what He does best. Let Him freely love you and set you once and for all *free* from this hurt.

> Dear Lord, please dress the wounds in my life, the self-inflicted ones as well as the ones inflicted by others. Give me the ability to forgive those in my past and those currently in my life, everyone who brought pain and hurt to me. Please reach out Your hand and not only heal me in Your timing and Your method, but also fill me with Your love to accept Your graciousness with thanksgiving. I reach out to You today; please accept my little faith. Stop my bleeding, dress my wound, and please, God, *heal me*. In Jesus' name, Amen.

I hope by now you are beginning to believe that not only can God heal your hurt, but also He can dress the wound so that a clean, healthy healing will take place.

God has made Himself available to all who hurt. In the Bible He has revealed His love, concern, and power for all of mankind. Remember, just as physical hurts require strong medicine and disinfectants, so do our personal hurts.

Jesus does not want us to suffer but to enjoy life to the max. Let the Holy Spirit take the words of Scripture to begin a new work within your heart. Let the Bible be an instrument in God's hand to bring you wholeness and health. Let God's virtue and power flow through the Holy Scriptures into your life and make you a new person, whole and fit for the King's service.

It is shocking to realize that the majority of people today simply endure the present while waiting for the future, waiting for something to happen, waiting for "next year," waiting for a better time, waiting for tomorrow. Many people are unable to see that all anyone ever has is today. Yesterday is gone; tomorrow exists only in hope.

Isn't it time for you to be released from the trap which snares you? Let God dress the wound in your life. It is imperative that you dress the wound, or it will fester more and more—and that which could be handled easily today will instead require prolonged and radical attention later, taking you far longer to heal than necessary. Why wait for a "better time"? There is no better time than now. It is God's plan that you start enjoying life. So why not cooperate with Him, starting this moment?

7

Develop
a Game Plan

The Tender Touch of God

After we assess the damage and stop the bleeding, we need a game plan to make sure that our problem can be brought under control. And one of the best ways to do that is to develop a game plan.

"Oh, no! Not a game plan!" you say. A game plan may bring images of a Super Bowl team memorizing plays for the big game. Or it may suggest seven-foot-tall NBA players kneeling down on the hardwood floor around their coach, looking at a white board marked up with X's and O's. But the kind of game plan I'm thinking of doesn't have anything to do with sports; it's just a workable blueprint that helps you to reach a desired goal. It does not mean more pain, although it may mean more discipline.

Do you know the Bible verse, "The joy of the LORD is your strength" (Nehemiah 8:10)? Let me put it this way: If you knew that a game plan was a) going to bring you strength; and b) going to bring you joy; wouldn't you say, "Yes, let's proceed"? Well, that's what God wants to do through a game plan. He wants to make dressing your wound into a joyful process that will ultimately strengthen you.

If we wait too long to develop such a game plan, a warped personality can set in. Oh, maybe not the extreme personality that we looked at in chapter 1; I'm not talking about becoming a Frankenstein or some ghoulish monster. But I am talking about being crippled in personal relationships.

Drugs are no substitute for a game plan. Many people are living off drugs prescribed to them legally by their physician, but their problems get no better. Drugs may allow them to mask their pain, but drugs will never eliminate the pain. They may even make the situation worse.

Let me give you a simple example of a game plan. Until recently, in my own life I did not have a game plan concerning physical pain. And it was killing me.

A Not-So-Amusing Ride

For the past few days as I've been working on this book, I've had to sit for hours typing on my MacIntosh (with a name like mine, what other kind of computer could I have?). This causes my back problems to flare up; all the sitting aggravates my condition. It's a vicious cycle that began five years ago at an amusement park.

It was our youngest daughter's fifteenth birthday. She wanted me to go with her on a ride that was guaranteed to be the experience of a lifetime (though not, I'm sure, a lifetime of pain). In this roller-coaster ride, each person was to sit on what resembled a bicycle seat. Then a solid harness was pulled over your head, locking your shoulders and upper torso in place. Once the ride began, you were riding what amounted to a roller coaster with no car to sit in.

Unfortunately, the upper-torso apparatus locked in before I was comfortably seated. The ride began anyway, and I found myself pushing with my feet in a squatting position and shrugging my shoulders upward as hard as possible to keep my balance and to resist the forces of the turns, spins, and bounces of the ride. Apparently, this caused my back muscles to spasm and lock up. It was a miserable experience.

Over the past five years my body must have masked the problems caused by this incident. In recent doctor's visits, I discovered I have three major back problems, each one aggravated by the others.

Apparently, the original trauma caused my back muscles to spasm and lock up in defense of my spine. Then over the next three years two discs began to get out of line and pinch my nerves, which in turn caused a chronic sprain to my lower back. All of this time the muscles were getting tighter and tighter, so that my back is in a constant state of tension.

I can honestly say that for the past three to four years I have never enjoyed a full eight hours of non-interrupted sleep. I never wake up rested and refreshed. It can get pretty discouraging.

Eight months ago I was a guest in Taiwan. My friend Luis Palau was holding evangelistic meetings in the stadiums of the six largest cities of Taiwan and had invited me to go ahead of him and meet with the Christian leaders of these cities and to speak in each city to churches, colleges, and at business luncheons.

The hectic schedule and the long airplane ride placed so much stress upon my back that I left two days early to return to San Diego and meet with the neurosurgeon. The pain was so intense, the discomfort level so high, that I was ready that day to have back surgery or whatever it would take to alleviate the pain. After a thorough examination and an MRI, we discovered the bulging discs.

I had placed myself into the surgeon's hands. Whatever he said, I would do. To my great relief, he said surgery was not necessary at this time. Instead, physical therapy and stretching exercises were recommended (this is what my family doctor had prescribed a year earlier). What a relief! Now at least I was sure of the problem. I could stop the bleeding and begin to dress the wound. Through the people who would help me, I was able to design a game plan. My rehabilitation—my game plan—has four facets:

1. Physical therapy twice a week, to begin the healing process and strengthen the lower back muscles. This will allow the two discs to return where they belong and take the pressure off the nerves.

2. Working out in the gym three times per week, to give my body both aerobic stamina and body strengthening.

3. A low-fat diet to reduce body weight and fat content. (This is the hardest . . . I love my cheeseburgers.)

4. A massage twice a week. Because I both sit and stand for hours each week, the problem increases rather than decreases. Hence the massage.

Without a game plan to change my lifestyle and a commitment to follow that plan, in ten years I would no doubt be a stooped, crippled old man.

Of course, it would be easy to take muscle relaxants. Yet I hate the hangover feeling they give me. It would be easy to drink a six-pack of beer each time the pain arrives; it would be simple to drink some wine or other alcoholic drink when the pain comes knocking every hour at my door. It definitely would be easier to live off Valium or other tranquilizers, but I don't want that lifestyle. I want an active life.

I have the world's greatest wife who loves me a zillion, and she needs all the love and fun I can give her. She deserves the best, not what's left. I have three sons and three daughters and five gorgeous granddaughters who need an active dad and grandpa. I like jet-skiing, four-wheeling, swimming, football, jogging, basketball, weight training. I refuse to give them up. I love life, and I love the people who are in my life.

So many times I've cried out to God and begged, "Please take this constant pain and discomfort away from me!" Yet it's still here, even as I type.

It may sound silly, but this game plan has introduced me to so many new people. Joyful relationships have been given to me. During the the past four days, I've had massage therapy three times. Mahina is a Hawaiian whose father had such serious back problems that he walked on his hands and knees. As she worked on my back and told me his story, I was so thankful that my pain was nothing compared to her father's. In each session, with her therapeutical skills at work, I've learned something new about my condition. I know that if I am diligent I will see my problems diminish and perhaps even go away. (By the way, her father's did.)

A while back, the therapist noted that my muscles are knotted up under my shoulder blades. After she finished working on them, I realized my posture was dictated by the limitation of my muscles. On the way home, I started yawning. After the fifth or sixth yawn, I realized these were deep, refreshing yawns. I couldn't remember how long it had been since I yawned this deeply; it reminded me of what it must have felt like to wake up in the morning and feel refreshed.

The next day I related this to the masseur, and she said it was because my rib cage was able to expand and the muscles stretched further than they had in a long time. This allowed my lungs to expand and take in more air, which in turn allowed me to feel better. The physical therapist has pointed out more than once that I breathe shallowly instead of deeply. Now I am taking in more air and feeling clearer in my mind. I know that I must keep my shoulders back so that my chest can take in more air. This can be a struggle, however, since my muscles are trained to allow my body to slump, giving me bad posture. It will take discipline in my life to retrain them and to remind them what normal really is.

Today I have a game plan, and regular massage is part of it. I didn't know that before. Now I realize it is part of the healing process.

I need this game plan, because if I let pain control my life, I lose. I miss out. I lose the joy of living and may wind up with a slightly warped personality. If I am not careful, those around me can suffer just as much as I do. I must realize that the fallout of my pain has ramifications for many people. That's why I'm so grateful for my new game plan.

Working on a Game Plan

You, too, need a game plan. Why? A game plan will keep you focused on the objective: Stop the bleeding, dress the wound, and let God heal. Remember, if you don't dress the wound *now*, you are in for bigger troubles later on in life.

A game plan is simply an approach to something you are trying to accomplish. In your game plan you need to know the strengths and weaknesses of your team, as well as those of your opponent. Your plan must be able to adjust to your opponent's game plan, too.

For example, if you are trying to lose weight, then your diet is a game plan. It might be a simple plan to cut out fats and lower your calorie intake on your own, or you might decide to call Jenny Craig or Weight Watchers who will help you set up a plan for yourself with some built-in accountability. Or maybe you can afford to do what Oprah Winfrey, the afternoon television talk-show host, did: Hire yourself a full-time cook who will control your food and your intake.

In business a game plan is known as a pro forma; in an English class it is an outline; in financial circles it is called a forecast or a budget.

I find that it is best to write down your game plan, rather than keep it in memory. Why? Because you can forget your commitment to help yourself. So write it down. Read it and pray over it. For some reason, putting it down on paper allows you to become bigger than what you have faced or are now facing. The problem becomes manageable.

The first thing to do in developing a game plan is to make sure you've stopped the bleeding. That is number one. Second, you want to dress the wound. There may be many steps required to do this. Your game plan might look something like this:

1. Stop the bleeding.
    a. Be honest.
    b. Talk with those involved.
    c. Communicate with godly friends.
    d. Call upon God.
2. Dress the wound.
    a. Seek counseling.
    b. Confess and repent, if necessary.
    c. Forgive those who wronged you;
       forgive yourself, if necessary.
    d. Commit your situation to God in prayer.
    e. Etc.

Of course, this is very basic and elementary; you will want to develop a more specific plan for your own needs, as I did for my back problems. The good news is, I am sure you will begin feeling positive change the moment you are able to identify and clarify your situation.

Your game plan may include a getaway or a trip to Hawaii to be in the sunshine. I don't know what it might be, because each one of us is different. Just begin where you are and look at the situation. Is your pain caused by the ultimate pain? Have you just broken up with your boyfriend, gotten a divorce, filed bankruptcy?

Whatever it is, develop a game plan to help you dress the wound. And don't forget: God must be central in the plan. He certainly knows the game of life better than anyone.

Learning from Elijah

A famous figure from the Old Testament may help us to think through an effective game plan. Elijah was an Old Testament prophet who performed many miracles. He was a fearless man when it came to proclaiming God's will to the people. In the following text, Elijah has just confronted King Ahab and his 450 prophets of Baal. They were all killed after Elijah confronted them on Mount Carmel. Ahab's wicked wife, Jezebel, apparently "wore the pants" in the royal family, and when she heard about what Elijah had done to her false prophets, she grew furious.

> And Ahab told Jezebel all that Elijah had done, and withal how he had slain all the prophets with the sword. Then Jezebel sent a messenger unto Elijah, saying, So let the gods do to me, and more also, if I make not thy life as the life of one of them by tomorrow about this time.
>
> And when he saw that, he arose, and went for his life, and came to Beersheba, which belongeth to Judah, and left his servant there. But he himself went a day's journey into the wilderness, and came and sat down under a juniper tree: and he requested for himself that he might die; and said, It is enough; now, O LORD, take away my life; for I am not better than my fathers.
>
> And as he lay and slept under a juniper tree, behold, then an angel touched him, and said unto him, Arise and eat. And he looked, and, behold, there was a cake baken on the coals, and a cruse of water at his head. And he did eat and drink, and laid him down again. And the angel of the LORD came again the second time, and touched him, and said, Arise and eat; because the journey is too great for thee. And he arose, and did eat and drink, and went in the strength of that meat forty days and forty nights unto Horeb the mount of God (1 Kings 19:1-8 KJV).

Of course, you and I are not mighty and illustrious prophets of old. Even so, God can use this story to help us develop an effective game plan.

First, notice that Elijah ran for his life. It's almost unfathomable to think that this man—who stood upon Mount Carmel and called for fire to fall from the sky; who saw God answer his prayer and send the fire that destroyed the offering and all that was around the altar; who stood fearless before 450 false prophets who screamed and shouted and cut themselves in front of the people of Israel; who challenged so many to test and prove their God—could wind up running away from a woman. Yet I guess running away is a natural response for all of us when confronted with the threat of death. As you begin to come up with a game plan, ask yourself a very important question: "Am I running?"

Second, note that although verse 3 tells us Elijah was traveling with a servant, apparently he left him in Beersheba and proceeded alone for another day. In other words, the prophet withdrew. It is natural for us to want to withdraw when we have been hurt. Yet in some cases, it is very important to have people around. It helps to have someone to talk to, to put his or her arms around you. As you begin to come up with a game plan, ask yourself a second very important question: "Am I withdrawing?"

Third, once alone, Elijah prayed to God that he might die. He was exhausted, he had drained his physical resources and strength. You see, after Elijah emerged victorious from his conflict with the priests of Baal, he prayed that a three-year drought would end. When God confirmed that a great storm was coming, Elijah sent his servant to tell Ahab to get into his chariot and hurry out of that area, or he would get stuck in the mud. Then Elijah ran several miles downhill and outran the king's chariot, beating him to the valley floor of Jezreel. Naturally, the prophet was physically worn out, as well as spiritually exhausted. He was also emotionally drained. The queen had publicly declared that he was a dead man, and the word was out, "If you don't want the queen's wrath, you'd better get rid of Elijah." To be physically, spiritually, and mentally exhausted is a dangerous place to be. When we are in this condition, we can make stupid decisions and say stupid things. As you begin to come up with a game plan, ask yourself a third very important question: "Am I physically, spiritually, or mentally exhausted?"

Fourth, Elijah sought death more than life. His circumstances and the pain he felt blocked out life and prompted him to embrace death. As you begin to develop your own game plan, ask yourself a fourth important question: "Am I blocking out life and embracing death?"

Fifth, Elijah fell asleep and God sent an angel to minister to him. That almost seems a little strange to us. If an angel appeared to us, wouldn't he do more than bring us a meal? Note that the angel said, "Wake up and eat." Elijah did just that, and after eating he fell back asleep. The angel later woke him a second time, and Elijah ate again. The words spoken to Elijah at this time are important for you and me: "Arise and eat; because the journey is too great for thee." Let these words sink in. The journey is also too great for you. You can't make it on your own energy. All of your strength may not be there for you at this time. You must invite God to help you to continue on living. As you begin to come up with a game plan, ask yourself a fifth very important question: "Am I eating and sleeping correctly? Am I depending on God's strength and not my own?"

The mere fact that you are willing to develop a game plan (as sketchy as it may be), is reassurance that you have finally stopped the bleeding and are now dressing the wound. If you will commit to developing a game plan, I know that you will win the game.

What's in Your Plan?

You can begin today to develop your game plan with a few simple words written down on paper or typed into your computer. What will your game plan be? What should be included?

Counseling should probably be one of the items in your plan. Rest should also be included, but some people hide under the covers when troubles hit them. Others might take sleeping pills and try to sleep away their problems. Too much sleep can be as damaging as too little sleep. What is it that you most need?

An eight-year-old was being interviewed on TV. The child came from a large family in which Mother got up first, sent the children off to school, hustled the father off to work, and then tackled her daily household chores. The child was asked, "What do you think your mother wants most?" The boy replied immediately, "To go back to bed."

Charles Swindoll, one of the premier American pastors of modern history, understands the importance of rest. He is a man who has studied hard, preached well, taught with discipline, overseen a congregation with integrity, and been a faithful husband and a dutiful father. Chuck is not only a gifted teacher but also a prolific writer.

Chuck writes, "Renewal and restoration are not luxuries; they are essentials. Being alone and resting for a while is not selfish. There is absolutely nothing enviable or spiritual about a coronary or a nervous breakdown, nor is an ultra busy schedule necessarily the mark of a productive life."[1] This quote reminds us that we need to include not only rest, but quiet times and reflective times as well. These will surely help to dress the wound.

Are you willing to take the necessary steps to dress the wound? If so, be sure to include in your game plan time for rest, quiet, solitude, reflection, and meditative time. Remember, we can learn things in the silence that we would never discover in the tumult of life.

A Long-Awaited Performance

Although I'm not sure where this story originates, it's a remarkable illustration of planning and perseverance. A piano teacher simply and affectionately known as Herman taught in a university's music department. One night at a concert, a distinguished piano player suddenly became ill while performing an extremely difficult piece. No sooner had the artist retired from the stage when Herman rose from his seat in the audience, walked onstage, sat down at the piano, and with great mastery completed the performance.

Later that evening at a party, a student asked Herman how he was able to perform such a demanding piece so beautifully without notice and with no rehearsal. He replied, "In 1939, when I was a budding young concert pianist, I was arrested and placed in a Nazi concentration camp. Putting it mildly, the future looked bleak. But I knew that in order to keep the flicker of hope alive that I might someday play again, I needed to practice every day. I began by fingering a piece from my repertoire on my bare-board bed late one night. The next night I added a second piece and soon I was running through my entire repertoire. I did this every night for five years.

"It so happens that the piece I played tonight at the concert hall was part of that repertoire. That constant practice is what kept my hope alive. Every day I renewed my hope that I would one day be able to play my music again on a real piano, and in freedom."

Herman had a game plan which he followed for many long years, in hope that one day he would be free again. It was that game plan that enabled him to do the seemingly impossible.

A game plan can do the same for you. An effective game plan, diligently carried out, can bring hope and eventual freedom. So take the plunge. Develop a game plan. And who knows? One day you may find yourself giving the performance of a lifetime.

8

The Importance of
Counselors

——The Tender Touch of God——

Counseling is often an effective way to "dress the wound" and let the healing process begin. And finding the right counselor is an invaluable key to a healthy recovery. God often uses people to help us recover from our wounds; but always, He is at the center of our healing. I know that firsthand.

Dead Man Walking

Dr. Sherwood Wirt wrote a book titled *For the Love of Mike*, which detailed God's work in my life from youth to 1983. In it he related the story of how God healed me. For the sake of time and space, I'll give you the condensed version here.

In the sixties when my generation was caught up in a cultural revolution, I too "experimented." One Sunday about 4 P.M. in sunny southern California, a friend handed me a pill and said, "Here, try this." Stupidly, I took it. Nothing happened the first four hours, then "all hell broke loose." Whatever this pill was, it scared me. I knew it was as bad as if I had been given poison.

About 8 P.M. I was in a house with eight or ten people I didn't really know. Our mutual friend had left me alone while he went to pick up his girlfriend. My mind seemed as if it was on fire. I sensed that this was serious, and that I had better get to a hospital quickly. I started to panic, the devil took over, and the people in that room played a sick game with me. They led me to believe that they were going to kill me.

Through the haze of a hallucination, I thought they had loaded a pistol, put a bag over my head, tied my hands behind my back, and put me down on the floor on my knees. I cried out to God to help me, but all I saw in my mind's eye was pitch blackness. Then Buddha, Maharishi, and Krishna all appeared and began to laugh at me. I had followed many young knowledge seekers into the Eastern religions and philosophies, and I had studied all the teachings of all three of these men. But now they all mocked me and said, "This is as far as we take man—DEATH!" I knew that my life was over . . . and my old Sunday school training reminded me that I was going to go to hell.

At that moment Jesus appeared, so brightly that all the demon apparitions disappeared. "Michael," He said, "you believed in Me, but you never received Me." I wept and ask God to forgive me of my sins and the wayward life I'd been living.

Now, I do not want to overdramatize this vision of Jesus or make you think that I had an Isle of Patmos revelation like the apostle John; I didn't. The vision was simple, peaceful, and terribly bright. But the next event was ugly.

To this day, 27 years later, I don't know what happened; but I thought I felt a gun to my head followed by an explosion. I thought my face had been blown off. I begged the people in the room to take me to the hospital because "I had a hole in my head." I remember the confused looks on everyone's faces, which leads me to believe that the event happened only inside my tortured brain.

The following week I turned myself in for observation at a local hospital to see if I was okay. I eagerly sought counseling; I wanted to be whole. I wanted to get on with my life and be productive. I was referred to a counselor who worked with me for ten months to help me realize that I hadn't really been shot and that I was alive. Then I spent seven months in group therapy, interacting with other people.

My problem was definitely unique to the group—they had never met a dead man before. It helped me to interact and realize, "Okay, I'm alive. But why does my face always disappear when I'm shaving? Why do I relive that explosion every night?" I didn't know it, but God already had a plan in place that would heal me—such a wonderful plan that He would use it to heal not just me, but thousands more.

The Jesus Movement had just begun, and I stuck my nose into the tent like a camel. Before I knew it, I was completely inside the tent. Jesus was moving, picking up all His little lambs who got lost in the hippie movement. Michael MacIntosh, fortunately, was on His list. I gave my heart to Jesus at Calvary Chapel in Costa Mesa, California. The Holy Spirit baptized me with God's love one evening, and I have never been the same man since.

One month later I attended the men's prayer meeting at Calvary. I walked to the front of the chapel and told Pastor Chuck Smith my story. I knew I was saved; I knew I was going to heaven. I just couldn't stop having these flashbacks. I still was not totally sure if this were a dream—or had I actually been shot and was living in hell?

Chuck and the church elders laid their hands on my head and shoulders and anointed me with oil as the Scriptures instructed them to do. Then Chuck prayed for me. As he prayed, I saw in my mind what appeared to be an electrical charge like a lightning bolt arcing from the left side of my brain to the right side. Then a small, still voice said, "Michael, I have not given you the spirit of fear; but of love, power, and a sound mind."

Instantly, I knew that I had been healed. That small, still voice quoted the Scripture from 2 Timothy 1:7. God had used the prayer of His minister, a verse from the Bible, and the miracle of the Holy Spirit to heal me of probable brain damage, both psychological and neurological. I dropped to the floor with my face on the carpet and wept. I knew that I knew I was healed. After two years of thinking I was dead, it was as if I woke up from an ugly nightmare. God had healed me!

Since then, I have never suffered a flashback or reoccurrence of those awful thoughts that the devil once used to try to destroy me. I know how fortunate I am, because millions of people have endured "bad trips," never getting over the flashbacks or regaining their right minds. Many are still in hospitals; others are simply nonproductive members of society, living off welfare checks. Still others overdosed and died, while others could not bear to live with so much pain and hurt and so committed suicide.

In the midst of my struggles, I sought counseling to dress the wound in my soul. I had a very sensitive psychologist who met with me every week for almost two years. He did all he could—but it was not enough. I ran up a big bill with him, but was unable to pay because I wasn't working at the time.

After giving my life to Jesus, I went back to his office to apologize to him and give him 10 dollars toward my account. He asked me to bring him up-to-date. I told him I was doing fine and that I had been born again. He asked me to explain what I meant. After listening to me, he said, "Michael, I am going to call the collection agency and tell them to cancel their action against you."

"But I want to slowly pay the bill off," I said.

"No," he replied, "it is obvious that something has happened to you that has changed your life for the better. And it is obvious it is not something I have done. You owe me nothing. I am very happy for you."

At the time of that conversation, I had been reading the Bible daily for three months and praying. God was fulfilling one of His tremendous titles—that of Wonderful Counselor.

The Wonderful Counselor

God is the One you want when it comes to good counsel. The following three passages make that abundantly clear.

> For unto us a child is born, unto us a son is given: and the government shall be upon his shoulder: and his name shall be called Wonderful, Counsellor, The mighty God, The everlasting Father, The Prince of Peace (Isaiah 9:6 KJV).
>
> Who hath directed the Spirit of the LORD, or being his counsellor hath taught him? (Isaiah 40:13 KJV).

> For I beheld, and there was no man; even
> among them, and there was no counsellor, that,
> when I asked of them, could answer a word
> (Isaiah 41:28 KJV).

These verses give us three potent reasons why we need good, healthy, biblical counseling.

First, in the prophecy of the birth of Christ in Isaiah 9:6, we are told that two aspects of His glorious name mean "wonderful" and "counselor." No one can give better counsel than He. He knows all about us and knows just what we need and how we need to receive it. His counsel is truly wonderful!

Second, always remember that God has no need for instructors; He does not have a Freudian foundation. He is the almighty, and since He made you, He is very capable of repairing your broken heart.

Third, remember that man often does not have the complete answer for your need. We need a good balance in counseling. God definitely does use godly men and women to give us advice, wisdom, and insight. But, ultimately, it has to be God's Word that places His tender touch on your soul. Please remember as you dress the wound to let godly counsel be a part of the medicine and bandaging. You can't get any better dressing for your wound.

The Ultimate Choice

The book of Judges tells how the tribe of Dan was seeking the right area in which to live. In that tribe was a man named Micah who had hired a young man to be his personal family priest. When the leaders of the Danites saw the priest, they said, "Ask counsel, we pray thee, of God, that we may know whether our way which we go shall be prosperous" (Judges 18:5 KJV). And the priest replied, "Go in peace: before the LORD is your way wherein you go" (Judges 18:6 KJV).

The Word of the Lord is the ultimate choice for counseling. It's crucial to hear what God has to say about your hurt. After all, He loves you more than anyone, and He knows the pain you feel. You will find that the Bible has thousands of soothing and comforting words which bring invaluable counsel.

We all know there are many people who will offer to "show you the way" . . . for 200 dollars an hour. The question that needs to be asked is this: Is the direction the counselor suggests the right way? Often turmoil in our lives spins us around and we feel disoriented. We must get good directions or we may remain lost for a long time.

I recently read a story about Fred Haynes, a pastor at Friendship Church in Dallas, who on a flight to Missouri was dismayed to find his seat in the economy section already occupied by another passenger. His concern quickly turned to elation when the flight attendant led him to a vacant seat in first class. Fred's delight was short-lived, however, when he discovered that the plane was headed to the wrong city and he would miss his speaking engagement. Later he reflected, "The devil is happy to give you a seat in first class, just so long as you're on the wrong plane."

So, too, must we be cautious in choosing a counselor. Some well-meaning people give counsel like a weather vane on top of a barn: They'll point you whichever way the wind happens to be blowing. The apostle Paul warned us about "winds of doctrine." We must be careful to seek out and heed solid, godly counsel. I know of at least one character in the Old Testament who would have profited from following this advice.

The Example of Naaman

Naaman was a prominent soldier who suffered from a skin disease (the King James version of the Bible calls it leprosy). He was not a Jew, yet he went to Israel to be cured. There he struggled with his emotions. As you read the story, it is easy to see that his personal pride, left unchecked, almost kept him from receiving his healing. His problem was that bigotry lived in his heart, masquerading as nationalism or patriotism. Read his story in 2 Kings 5:1-15 (KJV) and see if you can identify any of yourself there:

> Now Naaman, captain of the host of the king of Syria, was a great man with his master, and honourable, because by him the LORD had given deliverance unto Syria: he was also a mighty man in valour, but he was a leper (verse 1).

Notice the caliber of man Naaman was. Despite his strong leadership and heroic qualities, he had a physical impairment. The Hebrew word translated "leprosy" here was used for various diseases of the skin, not necessarily leprosy. But whatever the ailment was, whether leprosy or something else, it was a real trial to this man, which caused him much suffering:

> And the Syrians had gone out by companies, and had brought away captive out of the land of Israel a little maid; and she waited on Naaman's wife. And she said unto her mistress, Would God my lord were with the prophet that is in Samaria! for he would recover him of his leprosy (verses 2,3).

Isn't it beautiful, seeing this young woman sharing her faith with the wife of this national figure? When you believe in God, you should always share with others about God's love for people. Perhaps you have a friend at school or work who needs to know that God is alive and that He can cure hurts and pains. If so, won't you tell this person about Him?

> And one went in, and told his lord, saying, Thus and thus said the maid that is of the land of Israel. And the king of Syria said, Go to, go, and I will send a letter unto the king of Israel. And he departed, and took with him ten talents of silver, and six thousand pieces of gold, and ten changes of raiment. And he brought the letter to the king of Israel, saying, Now when this letter is come unto thee, behold, I have therewith sent Naaman my servant to thee, that thou mayest recover him of his leprosy.
>
> And it came to pass, when the king of Israel had read the letter, that he rent his clothes, and said, Am I God, to kill and to make alive, that this man doth send unto me to recover a man of his leprosy? wherefore consider, I pray you, and see how he seeketh a quarrel against me.
>
> And it was so, when Elisha the man of God had heard that the king of Israel had rent his clothes, that he sent to the king, saying, Wherefore hast thou rent thy clothes? let him come now to me, and he shall know that there is a prophet in Israel. So Naaman came with his horses and with his chariot, and stood at the door of the house of Elisha. And Elisha sent a messenger unto him, saying, Go and wash in Jordan seven times, and your flesh shall come again to thee, and thou shalt be clean.
>
> But Naaman was wroth, and went away, and said, Behold, I thought, He will surely come out to me, and stand, and call on the name of the LORD his God, and strike his hand over the place, and recover the leper (verses 4-11).

Here is a good lesson to be learned. As Peter said in Acts, "God is no respecter of persons" (see Acts 10:34 KJV). Naaman figured that since he was a big, important person on his side of the river, that everyone in Israel would treat him with the honor due someone of his stature. We, too, may be influential in our small circles; but in heaven, God is the center of attention. Note what Naaman said next:

> [Are] not Abana and Pharpar, rivers of Damascus, better than all the waters of Israel? may I not wash in them, and be clean? So he turned and went away in a rage (verse 12).

Here's that "nationalistic/patriotic" pride I wrote of earlier. Really, it is bigotry. He had Jews as his servants—why should he dunk himself in a Jewish river? But if he was to be healed, this pride had to go. God will not share His glory with anyone else:

> And his servants came near, and spake unto him, and said, My father, if the prophet had bid thee to do some great thing, wouldest thou not have done it? how much rather then, when he saith to thee, Wash, and be clean? (verse 13).

Fortunately for Naaman, his servants had wisdom that he couldn't deny. I think most of us are probably a little bit like Naaman. If the message is clothed in American Medical Association jargon or cloaked with big, long words and is given to us by a man or woman dressed in a white medical smock and a stethoscope around the neck, then it's got to be official. If the procedure is going to cost a lot of money, then it's got to be effective. Yet that is often the opposite of how God usually dresses the wounds of our lives. "'My thoughts are not your thoughts, nor are your ways My ways,' says the LORD. 'For as the heavens are higher than the earth, so are My ways higher than your ways, and My thoughts than your thoughts'" (Isaiah 55:8,9).

The mighty man from Syria should be grateful that his servants were able to talk some sense into their boss.

In the same way, our pragmatic and conservative minds need a jolt now and then to remind us that God is in control. Most of us seem to think that if God is in control, then there has to be some kind of big show, a major theatrical production accompanying what He does. That's certainly what Naaman thought. Yet God often acts not through fireworks and skywriting, but through quiet, ordinary measures. When Naaman finally calmed down enough to test the prophet's instructions, he found out the truth:

> Then went he down, and dipped himself seven times in Jordan, according to the saying of the man of God: and his flesh came again like unto the flesh of a little child, and he was clean (verse 14).

It was accomplished just as the prophet had said! No fireworks, no bolts from heaven. But when Naaman was willing to do what God had instructed, he received his healing. I don't know the method God may have in store for you, but believe me, God will act on your behalf if you just let Him go to work in His time and His way.

> And he returned to the man of God, he and all his company, and came, and stood before him: and he said, Behold, now I know that there is no God in all the earth, but in Israel (verse 15).

Naaman was grateful for what God had done for him. He wanted everyone to know that the God of Israel was truly the living God. Notice also that not only was the leprosy gone, but so was his pride and bigotry. Often God will use one issue in our lives just to deal with three or four more. Naaman was delivered from more than leprosy; he was given a soft and tender heart toward God.

Let God do this for you, too. He wants to dress your wound. Don't resist Him. It makes no sense.

Resisting the Touch of God

Nowhere do we see a better example of someone resisting God's healing hand than in the story of the man at the pool of Bethesda. The word *Bethesda* was of Aramaic origin. It meant "house of mercy" or "flowing water."

This pool was located near the sheep gate at Jerusalem. Because its waters had healing powers, the pool was visited by people from all around Israel, all hoping for a cure, a miracle. I am sure I would have been in the crowd looking for a healing. After all, testimony after testimony spread throughout Israel of the many people who had been cured. This is how John the apostle tells us it happened:

> Now there is at Jerusalem by the sheep market a pool, which is called in the Hebrew tongue Bethesda, having five porches. In these lay a great multitude of impotent folk, of blind, halt, withered, waiting for the moving of the water. For an angel went down at a certain season into the pool, and troubled the water: whosoever then first after the troubling of the water stepped in was made whole of whatsoever disease he had.
>
> And a certain man was there, which had an infirmity thirty and eight years. When Jesus saw him lie, and knew that he had been now a long time in that case, he saith unto him, Wilt thou be made whole? The impotent man answered him, Sir, I have no man, when the water is troubled, to put me into the pool: but while I am coming, another steppeth down before me. Jesus saith unto him, Rise, take up thy bed, and walk. And immediately

the man was made whole, and took up his bed, and walked: and on the same day was the Sabbath (John 5:2-9 KJV).

I've always found it interesting that in response to Jesus' question, the man had an excuse why he wasn't healed. Jesus wasn't interested in why he wasn't healed; He was simply interested in healing him. The man resisted the presence of God and tried to reason it out himself.

Could it be that you, too, are resisting and leaning on your own understanding? Could your pride be holding you back from the simplicity of trusting that God wants to dress up your hurts and make you whole?

Today is a great day to let God touch you. A new day, a new way. That's God's way. Maybe this is a good time for you to pray. Ask the Lord if there is any resistance to Him working in your life. Maybe the resistance is your pride. You are embarrassed to ask God to heal and bind up your hurt. You see yourself as a strong person and don't believe it would do any good to trust in God now. So many people over the years have told me that it isn't right that they've lived selfish lives and now, when they really need help, they call upon the Lord. They say it makes them feel like hypocrites. Why should God help them now?

Maybe you feel a little like that also. But that's only your pride. If God wants to forgive you and dress your wounds, that's His business, don't you think? Remember the old adage, "Don't look a gift horse in the mouth"? Well, it might just apply here, too. God's grace is a gift. Receive it with open arms—it is free, after all.

Go to the Lord

Several years ago author Dave Hunt wrote a best-selling book called *The Seduction of Christianity*. In the book he declares the great need for good, healthy,

God-inspired counseling. Mr. Hunt believes too many people are getting into kooky religions and offshoots of Christianity simply by failing to seek guidance from the Bible.

Knowing 2000 years ago that people would need directions for their lives, Jesus said, "I am the way, the truth, and the life. No one comes to the Father except through Me" (John 14:6). I urge you not only to find a godly, competent counselor, but also to consider getting counsel directly from God's Word.

The Bible is a great source for helping us find a cure for our problems, as varied and diverse as they may be. There is help for emotional, spiritual, and even mental disorders in the Bible. It contains stories of all kinds of people in every imaginable situation. These people's lives often parallel our own.

Often I have found that the story I happen to be reading at the time could just as easily be a story about me. The circumstances line up exactly with the circumstances I am facing. In fact, if I simply remove the name of the person suffering and slide mine in instead, the tale would fit my real-life experience to a tee. You will no doubt find the same is true for yourself.

9

Tapping into the
Power of God

The Tender Touch of God

When we hurt and are having a hard time finding help, one natural reaction is to pray—something I wholeheartedly endorse. Yet some Americans believe that it makes no difference if one prays or not. Even if they did pray, they say, they are unsure that God would hear them, let alone respond in their favor.

A survey by the Barna Research Group discovered that nearly 90 percent of Americans pray to God and 60 percent do so daily. Of those who pray, 61 percent make specific requests of God, and 46 percent listen silently for a personal response.[1]

The survey found that baby boomers (ages 28-46) and adult baby busters (the generation following) were less likely to engage in prayer or anticipate responses from God. Those who do not attend church pray less often and with less assurance; 63 percent of unchurched Americans pray regularly, compared with 82 percent of all Americans; and only 34 percent of the unchurched are certain that prayer makes a difference—a rate 22 percentage points lower than that of all Americans.

"Born-again" respondents, the poll said, were most likely to "see God as worthy of their praise (84 percent to 54 percent), as able to forgive them of their sins (86 percent to 68 percent), and as personally responding to their prayers (68 percent to 55 percent)." Those who did not view God in these ways continued to pray—even regularly—but their prayers reflected "thanksgiving rather than an entire range of ways of interacting with God," Barna said. Of all participants, 95 percent who pray thank God, and 76 percent ask Him to forgive specific sins.

A Misunderstood Gift

Prayer is one of the most misunderstood and misdirected gifts that the Creator of mankind has given His children. Prayer, correctly directed, is the best recourse we have when faced with crisis and hurt. It is the divine resource that allows comfort, understanding, and acceptance to flow through our lives during our most difficult times.

For years I have been praying for the opportunity to preach the gospel to one million people in Tiananmen Square in Beijing, China. I spoke to Bishop Teng at dinner one evening in Nanjing about this. He said, "Not today, Michael, but maybe some day." It would be wonderful to do it, and even better if I could speak Chinese. The best I have learned so far is, "Hello, how are you?" and "Thank you." The language seems so complex and so difficult to read or speak. Why, just the inflection of your voice in pronouncing a word can get you either a handshake or a slap in the face.

I have learned that the Chinese language features a suggestive and challenging word which is usually translated into English by the term "crisis." The word is written by combining two characters, one for "danger" and the other for "opportunity." The term is pronounced *way gee* and means a "dangerous opportunity."

The pain and hurt in your life might have been brought on by a crisis, but what a shift of thinking it would be to look at your situation as a *way gee*. This dangerous situation you face is really an opportunity. And the best way to seize the opportunity is to pray and see what heaven has to say about it.

Heaven's doors are always open for prayers. Bob Dylan sang a song which repeats over and over: "Knock, knock, knocking on heaven's door." God's response is, "Come on in, the door's open." Let's take a peek inside heaven through the Scriptures and see what your prayers look like coming up from earth.

A Peek Inside Heaven

The Bible is filled with scriptures about prayer and the power of answered prayer. God wants you to use this prayer power to draw closer to Him and learn of His love for you. Prayer is a powerful key to healing. James thought it was so important that he ended his epistle by telling the Christian community what to do about their pain, illness, sickness, and afflictions:

> Is any among you afflicted? let him pray. Is any merry? let him sing psalms. Is any sick among you? let him call for the elders of the church; and let them pray over him, anointing him with oil in the name of the Lord: And the prayer of faith shall save the sick, and the Lord shall raise him up; and

if he has committed sins, they shall be forgiven
him. Confess your faults one to another, and pray
one for another, that ye may be healed. The effec-
tual, fervent prayer of a righteous man availeth
much (James 5:13-16 KJV).

According to these verses, there is much that we can
do to receive our healing. We can pray, confess our sins,
pray for others, call for the elders, be prayed for, be
anointed with oil, and have hands laid on us. That's a
handful right there. Prayer works, and prayer will give
you great inner strength and deepen your relationship
with God. God is the great healer, and He will listen to
you as you pray. Remember, it was Jesus who said:

Your Father knoweth what things ye have need
of, before ye ask him (Matthew 6:8 KJV).

Ask, and it shall be given you; seek, and ye shall
find; knock, and it shall be opened unto you
(Matthew 7:7 KJV).

And all things, whatsoever ye shall ask in prayer,
believing, ye shall receive (Matthew 21:22 KJV).

And whatsoever ye shall ask in my name, that
will I do, that the Father may be glorified in the
Son (John 14:13 KJV).

If you and I can't trust the words of Jesus, then we
are in real trouble. And yet if we can trust them completely—as we can—then we have real help for our
troubles.

Our prayers are vitally important to God. They are
precious to Him, and He takes them far more seriously
than we can ever imagine. The book of Revelation gives
us some interesting insights into how God views our
prayers:

> And when he had taken the book, the four beasts and four and twenty elders fell down before the Lamb, having every one of them harps, and golden vials full of odours, which are the prayers of saints (Revelation 5:8 KJV).

> And another angel came and stood at the altar, having a golden censer; and there was given unto him much incense, that he should offer it with the prayers of all saints upon the golden altar which was before the throne. And the smoke of the incense, which came with the prayers of the saints, ascended up before God out of the angel's hand (Revelation 8:3,4 KJV).

These verses picture our prayers as captured in golden vials in heaven. The prayers of the saints are immensely precious to God. These vials are described in the original Greek as "broad, shallow basins" or "deep saucers." How wonderful to know that sometimes our prayers are short and to the point; they may fill a shallow basin. On the other hand, that basin is wide and is capable of handling the many short prayers we may have for the Lord. The deep saucer tells us there may be times when we need to go longer and deeper in our prayers to the Lord.

What a glorious picture we glimpse here. Angels, music, aromatic fragrance, golden utensils—it's something to ponder. Just think: Your prayers are so important that they receive royal treatment, being personally delivered to God Himself. This in itself is a reason to start praying today.

How Soon Will My Prayers Be Answered?

How long does it take for our prayers to make it to heaven? We can begin answering that question by looking into the prayer life of a great statesman and prophet named Daniel. Prayer was an integral part of his daily life. Even Daniel's enemies knew that he was a man of prayer. In fact, the leaders of Babylon came to King Darius with a plan whose intent was kept from the king. They flattered the king and said, "Whosoever shall ask a petition of any God or man for thirty days, save of thee, O king, he shall be cast into the den of lions" (Daniel 6:7 KJV). The Scriptures go on to say concerning this plot:

> Now when Daniel knew that the writing was signed, he went into his house; and his windows being open in his chamber toward Jerusalem, he kneeled upon his knees three times a day, and prayed, and gave thanks before his God, as he did aforetime.
>
> Then these men assembled, and found Daniel praying and making supplication before his God (Daniel 6:10,11 KJV).

Daniel didn't allow anything or anyone to come between him and his daily communication with God. No doubt you know the rest of the story. The conspirators had readied a den of lions to eat anyone who dared disobey the king. Of course, they insisted that King Darius make no exceptions and throw his loyal servant to the lions. Reluctantly, he did so. But after a night in the lions' den, Daniel prevailed and told the king that God had sent an angel from heaven to shut the mouths of the lions.

Isn't it wonderful to know that praying men have a faithful God looking after them? No matter what the odds may be against us, God will intercede and prevail on behalf of His children.

Later in Daniel's life, prayer again brings him through some tough times. In chapter 9 we are told of a visit by the great angel Gabriel:

> And while I was speaking, and praying, and confessing my sin and the sin of my people Israel, and presenting my supplication before the LORD my God for the holy mountain of my God; Yea, whiles I was speaking in prayer, even the man Gabriel, whom I had seen in the vision at the beginning, being caused to fly swiftly, touched me about the time of the evening oblation. And he informed me, and talked with me, and said, O Daniel, I am now come forth to give thee skill and understanding. At the beginning of thy supplications the commandment came forth, and I am come to shew thee; for thou art greatly beloved: therefore understand the matter, and consider the vision (Daniel 9:20-23 KJV).

How wonderful to see that prayer can move God to send angels to encourage us! Gabriel tells us in verse 23 that it was at the beginning of Daniel's supplication that God sent him forth.

Now let's look at one more instance of Gabriel coming to Daniel. It is found in chapter 10:

> Then said he unto me, Fear not, Daniel: for from the first day that thou didst set thine heart to understand, and to chasten thyself before thy God, thy words were heard, and I am come for thy words. But the prince of the kingdom of Persia withstood me one and twenty days: but, lo, Michael, one of the chief princes, came to help me; and I remained there with the kings of Persia (Daniel 10:12,13 KJV).

Verse 12 tells us that God responded to Daniel's prayers the first day he asked for help. That is how quickly you can expect a response from God. Notice I said *response*, not *answer*. Sometimes we may not see the answer to our prayers for a while, but that does not mean God hasn't responded.

Verse 13 tells us of a demonic interception of Gabriel. Somewhere between God's throne room and Daniel's prayer room, the devil tried his best to keep heaven from getting to earth. In the end, Gabriel defeated this "prince of Persia" and delivered his message to Daniel. We should always remember that the devil is real and will try to use delayed answers to prayer in order to keep you from God. But in the end, God always gets His help through. Prayer brings you tremendous heavenly support. Feel free to use it more often.

Journey into the World of Prayer

Many people think prayer is a ritual. Yet if that were true, then prayer would be something only for priests, pastors, and holy men. Clearly, it is much more than that. A story that I heard illustrates this.

During World War II, a young soldier fighting in Italy jumped into a foxhole just ahead of some bullets. Immediately, he tried to deepen the hole for more protection and was frantically scraping away the dirt with his hands. While digging, he unearthed something metal and brought up a silver crucifix, left behind by a former resident of the foxhole. A moment later another man leaped into the foxhole and landed beside him as the shells screamed overhead. When the soldier got a chance to look, he saw that his new companion was an army chaplain. Holding out the crucifix, the soldier gasped, "Am I glad to see you! How do you work this thing?"

Do you ever feel like that soldier? "How do I work this thing called prayer?" It is simple. Let me suggest five very easy steps to enable you to begin your journey into the world of prayer. It's time for you to begin moving along your road toward healing.

1. *Recognize that prayer is communication.*

When you communicate, you do two things. You speak and you listen. Prayer is the same way. It is two-way communication, not one-way. Many people think prayer is talking to God. That's only half right. Effective prayer includes listening to God, too.

People pray because of great joy, great sadness, and despondency. Prayer is communication—real and genuine communication between a person and God. I encourage you to read the Psalms, which are full of prayers, and find role models for yourself. In fact, while you read particular psalms, do so with prayer. You will be amazed at the amount of solace and comfort you will find, see, and hear.

2. *Engage in prayer from your heart.*

Jesus said, "God is Spirit, and those who worship Him must worship in spirit and truth" (John 4:24). How would you feel if your children talked to you with no emotion? Or expressed their requests to you as if they were talking to a brick wall?

The Bible says that God knows what we need even before we ask. So be honest with Him. Do not be afraid to cry or sing or laugh. Prayer is from the heart. Be real with yourself, and you will be real with God.

3. *Prayer is not a ritual, so there is no specific body position for prayer.*

Some believe that in order to pray they must kneel. Others think they must be standing. You may think your hands need to be folded and you must be seated upright.

Remember when Jesus was walking on the water in the midst of a storm? Peter cried out, "If that's You, Lord, invite me out there to be with You." Jesus told Peter to join Him. But as Peter took a few steps, he took his eyes off Jesus and began to sink. What followed was possibly one of the shortest prayers in history: "Save me!" Peter cried. And do you know what? His prayer was heard and answered.

4. *There is no single "right" time to pray.*

The apostle Paul taught that we should "pray without ceasing" (1 Thessalonians 5:17). Some people think that God is too busy to have us pray too often. Or some may think that prayer is good only at mealtime, when we get into a tough situation, or at night when we go to sleep.

There was a little boy who, like many young children, was accustomed to having a night-light in his bedroom. His parents finally decided he was old enough to sleep in the dark. His mother told him about their decision, tucked him in, turned out the light, and began leaving the room. Out of the dark, he called out, "Do I have to, Mommy?" She told him, "Yes, darling, you're a big boy now." There was a pause, then he replied, "Well, then, may I get up and say my prayers again—louder?"

That little boy thought his prayers would be more effective if given more volume. But God is not deaf, nor does He sleep. He hears our prayers whenever we pray, as long as those prayers are sincere.

5. *There are no "required" words for your prayers.*

Recently, Sandy and I attended the memorial service of a lifelong friend. The minister read his prayers, reminding me that many Protestant and Catholic services have a standard prayer or liturgy for each ceremony and rite.

Can God answer liturgical prayers? Sure He can. But I also believe He has more room to pour out heaven's blessings when prayer is from the heart. You know your own pain. You know the loss and loneliness. You know if you are hurt, angry, disappointed, or even at a loss for words. God knows very well how you feel, so tell Him about it in truthful words. Could it be that you just don't understand why this had to happen to you? You don't know why God allowed this or that situation to arise? Then tell Him about it. You never have to worry that you will anger Him by being truthful about your emotions. In fact, when you get it all off of your chest, you will be surprised at the answers you discover through prayer.

Unfamiliar Territory

It's possible you aren't familiar with prayer. Prayer is simple. It is productive. It gets results. It works. You may say, "I don't know God. How can I talk to Him?" Actually, it is very simple.

If you were shopping for some new shoes and found a pair that you liked, wouldn't you walk up to a salesperson and ask for help? If you were in a new neighborhood and couldn't find the address you were looking for, wouldn't you ask a police officer or someone on the street for help? If you were in a library looking for research material, isn't the librarian the first person you would go to for help?

In all of these instances, the procedure is basically the same: The people you talk to are strangers. You've had no previous interaction with them, but you are willing to talk with them to help you achieve your goal.

How much more with God! Just begin talking; He's listening. Isaiah the prophet wrote these words from God: "Behold, the LORD's hand is not shortened, that it cannot save; neither his ear heavy, that it cannot hear" (Isaiah 59:1 KJV). He is listening, and He wants to hear from you.

Take time to stop and pray right now—quietly, reverently and ask the Lord to come to you with His comfort that the Scripture has promised. Let Him begin this very moment to begin dressing the hurt so that He can heal you.

Whatever You Do, Pray!

One day I asked Billy Graham about his personal prayer life. He told me that God had taught him to pray all day long. In the shower, driving in an automobile, flying in an airplane. In fact, he said that he had been asking God for wisdom while talking to me. He wanted to know what he could say or do to encourage me. Basically, he prayed unceasingly. Then, of course, there were prayers for Ruth. And there were times when he and Ruth would kneel beside the bed and specifically pray for one another and pray for their five children and numerous grandchildren.

This was the same answer my pastor, Chuck Smith, had given me as a young intern pastor. Pray unceasingly, pray specifically—but above all, pray.

Martin Luther once said:

> It is well to let prayer be the first employment in the early morning and the last in the evening. Avoid diligently those false and deceptive thoughts which say, *I will pray an hour hence; I must first perform this or that.* For with such thoughts a man quits prayer for business, which lays hold of and entangles him so that he comes not to pray the whole day long.

My grandmother was a very strong Christian woman. She lived to be 86 years old and was a gifted intercessor. She had a prayer group in her home every week. About four years after she died, I was preaching at a Bible study in Palm Springs, California. An elderly woman came up to me afterward and asked if I was raised in Oregon. "Yes, I was." Then she wanted to know if I had a grandmother who lived in Eugene, Oregon. "Why yes, I did. Why do you ask?" She told me that she belonged to my grandmother's Wednesday morning prayer meeting and that they used to pray for me. Here I was teaching the Bible years later—a long time after those dear ladies prayed. Nevertheless, their prayers were answered!

Before she died, my grandma asked me to promise that I would "give the gospel" to my Uncle George. Uncle George and I had never been close. He was an extremely successful businessman who early in life had departed from his mother's faith and her desire that he become a minister and follow in his father's footsteps. I promised Grandma I would talk to Uncle George about the Lord, but I never dreamed I would begin fulfilling that promise at the first funeral service I ever conducted—*her* funeral service. I preached the gospel, but Uncle George didn't respond.

The second opportunity to "give the gospel" to Uncle George came at his aunt's funeral. Again, no response. By this time I felt that I had kept my obligation to Grandma, even though I saw no fruit. Little did I realize the power of that woman's prayers, even after she had departed planet Earth and gone to heaven.

One day I visited Uncle George in his home, about 100 miles from my own. He was recovering from surgery, and since I was in the area, I called him as a favor to my mother. He invited me to come by and see him.

During my childhood, Uncle George was a frightening figure for me. He stood over six feet tall, with a large frame and the serious, regal bearing of a vice president of a large national firm. He was "the rich uncle"; I was the boy who lived in government housing. I never had much interaction with him over the years, so this lone trip to his house was a bit tense for me.

Yet I began to understand this man as I sat and listened to him talk. Now retired and in his sixties, he was charming, highly intelligent, and quite gentle and personable. I liked him. Then, quite unexpectedly, the conversation swung toward something that obviously had been on his mind for some time.

"Mike, because I know your past, I am very interested in what made you become a minister. You know, my father was a minister, and he died at the age of 26. Your grandmother always wanted me to grow up to be a minister. Please tell me about it."

This time I wasn't standing behind a pulpit in a mortuary; I was less than five feet away, sitting in his kitchen. Grandma's prayers had something to do with this meeting, I was sure.

I began by describing my childhood (which he knew), then my teen years and my early twenties. I repeatedly confessed how lost and confused I was, how I wanted to be like the other kids who had a dad. I described the anger and bitterness that filled my young heart.

Then I told him about Sandy and her love for me. I described her family and how they loved me, how her father was every bit as successful as Uncle George. I explained that on my own I could do nothing, and the marriage fell apart. When I got to the part about Jesus Christ coming into my life, he interrupted and said, "I remember these things about Jesus from Sunday school." George had been a tough businessman who let his wife see to the religious education of the children, so he wasn't terribly interested in the religious part of my story. Soon our conversation came to an end. On the drive home, I thought I had finally filled my obligation to Grandma, even though Uncle George remained in his sins.

A few years after my meeting with Uncle George, he called me. He asked if I would meet him for lunch halfway between our homes. During lunch he paused and said, "Mike, would you tell me what it means to be 'born again?'" I was amazed. Slowly I explained chapter 3 of the Gospel of John to him, where Jesus said a man must be born again to enter the kingdom of God.

When I finished, it was time for dessert. We talked for a few more minutes, then after the bill was paid and the table cleared, George the executive brought out a notepad and said, "Please tell me those Scripture references again. And once more tell me what it means to be born again."

On the way home I was amazed at how open and hungry this man was to be sure of eternal life. In his mother's eyes he had strayed from the "straight and narrow," gone off to big business and big money, and lost his soul. Finally, I truly had fulfilled my obligation to Grandma.

Shortly after our luncheon, Uncle George had a heart attack. He was in the intensive-care unit in a coma. After his funeral service a few days later, I realized that Grandma had asked Jesus over and over and over for many years to save her strong, intelligent son. It didn't happen in her lifetime, but it did happen in her grandson's. God worked through three generations to bring closure to one woman's faithful prayers.

Give Prayer a Chance

During the 1960s, John Lennon had divorced his wife, Cynthia, and married a Japanese artist named Yoko Ono. On their honeymoon they held press conferences from their bed in the Amsterdam Hilton Hotel. The Vietnam War was still in full swing, there was rioting on college campuses, and cities in Europe and the United States were battling disgruntled workers and students. John wrote a song as a theme for his message called "Give Peace a Chance."

After becoming a Christian, I designed a bumper sticker that had a picture of a dove with an olive branch in his bill and the words "Give Jesus a Chance." Today I would like to modify that and say, "Give Prayer a Chance." It really does work, especially when it's addressed to the great healer of our souls.

10

Clean
at Last

—The Tender Touch of God—

In 1842 the first bathtub was denounced as a "luxurious and democratic vanity." Boston made it unlawful to bathe, except on a doctor's prescription. In 1843 Philadelphia made bathing illegal between November 1 and March 15. (Given these laws, perhaps we can see why it was so popular in the last century to "Go West, young man"!)

These silly laws remind me of the conduct of a large number of people today. When in need of a deep spiritual cleansing, many people would rather put up with their stench of unconfessed sins than come clean before God. They would rather wallow in their own sinful filth than enjoy the healthy and invigorating washing of God. Yet they will never find healing that way. And they will never be released from their hurt.

Many of us are like the little boy who broke the glass of a street lamp. Greatly disturbed, he asked his father, "What shall I do?" "Do?" exclaimed his father. "Why, we must report it and ask what you must pay, then go and settle it." This practical way of dealing with the matter was not what the boy was looking for, and he whimpered, "I . . . I thought all I had to do was ask God to forgive me."

If we want to find healing and relief from many of the hurts that afflict us, we ourselves have an important part to play in the process. We must help to dress our wound. And sometimes in treating our wounds the most helpful action we can take is confession and repentance.

Little by Little

Sin doesn't usually happen all at once. Normally, there is a progression to sin. Sin eats away at us inside before any blemish shows. Sin takes its toll before the blemish is seen by our neighbors. Usually, it accomplishes its goal before it is seen. James 1:13-15 (KJV) says:

> Let no man say when he is tempted, I am tempted of God: for God cannot be tempted with evil, neither tempteth he any man: But every man is tempted, when he is drawn away of his own lust, and enticed. Then when lust has conceived, it bringeth forth sin: and sin, when it is finished, bringeth forth death.

Sin is always so easy to blame on someone else, isn't it? But God doesn't accept that at all. We are to blame for our sin, not someone else. James said we are drawn away of "our own lust." Then when we are hooked, lust conceives and gives birth to sin. Then the sin eats away at us like a cancer, like a deadly disease. The final step is death.

Earlier today I was listening to a Bible study on the radio. The teacher told how he had suffered an accident and went to the doctor to be treated. In setting up the next appointment, he was told he would have to wait a few days because his doctor was going to have a black mole on his stomach checked out. Three weeks later when the man called for an appointment, the receptionist told him the doctor had died. Apparently, when the specialist had opened up the doctor, he immediately sewed him right back up. The doctor was told to get his business in order because he was filled with cancer; he died two days later. He was 38 years old.

That's how it is with sin. Sin doesn't care what gender you are. It doesn't care if you are single or married, young or old. Sin is no respecter of persons. We may not see the damage it is doing inside our lives, then one day we see something out of the ordinary on the surface. But it doesn't appear to be anything but a blemish, so we overlook it. Others see the blemish and ignore it also. Why not? Everyone in the neighborhood has some sort of blemish. It is acceptable to our neighbors, but sin is never acceptable to God. Eventually—and perhaps sooner than later—that blemish shows itself for what it truly is. And all too quickly we discover our time is up.

If your relationships have gone sour, your business is going bad, your marriage is a disaster, could some of it be your fault? Is it possible that greed got the best of you? That you took advantage of someone for self-gain? That you have been a bully? If so, you need to recognize that you have sinned, and you must do two things where sin is concerned.

Confess Your Sin

First, you need to *confess* your sin. What does that mean? Simply admit your fault to God. Telling God that you sinned isn't going to surprise Him. He already knows what you have done. Confession shows your respect and submission to God—and the relief that comes with confession is overwhelming.

At the close of a sermon one Sunday, a man came forward at the invitation for people to pray and confess their sin. He was noticeably disturbed and moved by the conviction of sin in his life. With tears flowing and a wavering voice, he took the pastor's hand and meant to tell him that his life was full of sin. But what came out was, "My sin is full of life." As soon as he had spoken, he realized his mistake and changed it; but in reality, his first statement was the reason for the second. His sin was full of life and that is why his life was full of sin. The first step to dealing with that sin is to confess it. We can thank God that the blood of Jesus Christ is the complete remedy for sin.

When we look the Lord in the face and admit our sin, it is like the dressing of a wound. A curative has been applied to stop further damage. We assess the problem and then commit it to the Lord. Unless you've experienced it, it seems too hard to believe. Yet millions of people worldwide every day confess their sin to the Lord and experience this freshness.

The apostle John promised that "if we *confess* our sins, he is faithful and just to forgive us our sins, and to cleanse us from all unrighteousness" (1 John 1:9 KJV). The word "cleanse" in this scripture again paints for us the picture of dressing our wound. In a moral sense, it means "to free from guilt of sin" and "to purify." If you can evaluate your situation clearly, see if sin is plaguing your life. If so, confess it. Then God can cleanse this wound with the healing balm of forgiveness.

You may be struggling at this point because you can't get yourself to admit you are wrong. Charles Colson's book *Born Again* details his experiences during Watergate. In the book, Colson describes one of President Nixon's problems: He could never admit he was wrong about anything. In fact, Colson said that even when Nixon obviously had a cold—nose running, face red, sneezing, all the symptoms of a cold—he would never admit it.

Don't follow his example. Don't resist the truth that is shining in your heart right now. Confess your sin and take the responsibility that is yours. I won't deny that it may hurt a little, but I can guarantee that it will save a flood of hurt later on.

Recently, a huge tree in Colorado fell to the ground with a resounding crash after having stood majestically on a hill for more than 400 years. A mere sapling when Columbus landed in San Salvador, over the centuries it had been struck by lightning 14 times, braved great windstorms, and even defied an earthquake. In the end, however, it was killed by some little beetles. Boring under the bark, they chewed away its mighty fibers until one day that lordly king of the forest came thundering down.

So, too, apparently insignificant sins often make substantial inroads into our spiritual lives. If left unchecked, they may cause our downfall. You may not see any problem when you make your choice at 18 to start drinking; but you can see the fruit at 34 when you are an alcoholic. You may not realize the damage when you decide at 16 to be sexually promiscuous, but the fruit of that choice will reveal itself in your doctor's office at 29. The unseen destruction is invisible to you at 25 when you decide to stop going to church, but your hardened heart will manifest itself at 51 when you are in the hospital and the priest comes to stand beside your bed to administer last rites.

Repent of Your Sin

Second, we must be sure to *repent* of our sins. Repentance is more than just being sorry. Repentance involves both remorse or contrition for past conduct or sin, and the determination to turn from that sin today and in the future.

Repentance is more than just being sorry. Real repentance involves a change of attitude and action. One of America's finest Bible expositors, Donald Grey Barnhouse, told of a Sunday school class where the children were asked what was meant by the word *repentance*. A little boy put up his hand and said, "It is being sorry for your sins." A little girl also raised her hand and said, "It is being sorry enough to quit."

The third chapter of Acts tells how Peter and John went up to the temple in Jerusalem. This short story gives us some very good insight into confession and repentance:

> Now Peter and John went up together into the temple at the hour of prayer, being the ninth hour. And a certain man lame from his mother's womb was carried, whom they laid daily at the gate of the temple which is called Beautiful, to ask alms of them that entered into the temple; who seeing Peter and John about to go into the temple asked an alms.
>
> And Peter, fastening his eyes upon him with John, said, Look on us. And he gave heed unto them, expecting to receive something of them. Then Peter said, Silver and gold have I none; but such as I have give I thee: In the name of Jesus Christ of Nazareth rise up and walk. And he took him by the right hand, and lifted him up: and

immediately his feet and ankle bones received strength.

And he leaping up stood, and walked, and entered with them into the temple, walking, and leaping, and praising God. And all the people saw him walking and praising God: and they knew that it was he which sat for alms at the Beautiful gate of the temple: and they were filled with wonder and amazement at that which had happened unto him.

And as the lame man which was healed held Peter and John, all the people ran together unto them in the porch that is called Solomon's, greatly wondering (verses 1-11 KJV).

Peter didn't want the people worshiping him. Instead, he pointed the people to God. He told the crowds,

Repent ye therefore, and be converted, that your sins may be blotted out, when the times of refreshing shall come from the presence of the Lord; and he shall send Jesus Christ, which before was preached unto you (verses 19,20).

There's our word: *Repent* and be converted so your sins may be blotted out. That term "blotted out" is very strong in the original language. It literally means "to anoint or wash in every part." Sometimes it was used to mean "obliterate, erase, wipe out, or blot out." We must never lose sight of the finished work that God does when we repent of our sin. He obliterates it so that it is totally erased.

If your wound is caused by sin and you are willing to repent, then be assured that God is willing to forgive and erase the record that you ever committed such an act.

True repentance is far different from merely being sorry that you got caught. When the evangelical community was shocked by the scandals of Jim Bakker and

Jimmy Swaggart back in the eighties, radio talk-show host Larry King commented on the revelations concerning Swaggart:

> I would buy all of the sadness and tears and recriminations if, and this is a big if, Jimmy had come forward with his problem before somebody had pictures proving it. Anybody can be repentant when caught. Also, if he really wanted true forgiveness he could donate his estate and all that property to some worthy charity. Give up all his earthly goods. As Lenny Bruce once told me, "If Jesus Christ came back, he wouldn't own more than one suit as long as somebody in the world had no clothes."[1]

Remember what Peter had to say about the act of repentance? He chose three unique words to show that God is willing and able to dress our wounds. Note these three: *times, refreshing* and *presence.*

The term for *time, kairos,* means "a fixed and definite time, the time when things are brought to crisis, the decisive epoch waited for."

The word chosen for *refreshing, anapsuxis,* is used only once in the New Testament. It simply means "a cooling or a refreshing."

The word chosen for *presence* has a somewhat different meaning than does our English word. *Prosopon* is a Greek term used for the face or the front of the human head. It was often used when speaking of the countenance or look of a person, or the appearance one presents because of great wealth or high rank.

It appears that Peter is trying to emphasize that when we repent, a specific refreshing and cooling, soothing experience comes to us.

When we repent of our sins, the cleansing blood of Jesus does a deep penetration into that area of hurt that the best of analysts could never reach. Perhaps in your case it's an area which you have closed off for a long, long time. Light is now being shed upon it. The light of truth. Let the Holy Spirit help you dress the wound.

As one saint said,

> Repentance means that I own responsibility for my part in what was unsatisfactory behavior. I accept responsibility for my part in what is and what will be new behavior. Repentance is owning responsibility for what was, accepting responsibility for what is, and acting responsibly now.
>
> It is responsible action. It is not a matter of punishing ourselves for past mistakes, hating ourselves for past failures, or depressing ourselves with feelings of worthlessness.
>
> Repentance is finishing the unfinished business of my past and choosing to live in new ways that will not repeat old, unsatisfactory situations. In the full Christian meaning of the word, repentance is a process. It is a thawing out of rigid lifestyles into a flowing, moving, growing, repenting process.[2]

The biggest difficulty with repenting is that you and I cannot change ourselves. Only God can change us. That's why we must trust the Bible and rely on the person of the Holy Spirit to enable us to repent. Only through the power of the Spirit can we turn from our sin and walk in a direction that pleases God. Without His power, we are just religious people. True, we may be nice and good people, but that is not what God is after. He is after "a spiritual house, a holy priesthood" (1 Peter 2:5). And the only way that happens is through faith by the power of the Spirit.

No Time like the Present

If you need to confess and repent of some sin that has wounded you, let's do exactly as we have before. Let's pray and trust God that He will work a miracle. Refreshment will come to you as you pray and acknowledge the problem. Remember, if you seek His face, that which you desire most is going to be given to you. The guilt will be washed away, like germs from an open wound. A cooling, calm sense of peace will flood your soul as you let go and let God.

A simple prayer like the following can do wonders for your hurt today. Even as you pray, know that God is cleansing your wound and dressing it:

> Father, please forgive me of my sin. I realize that my life has progressed in such a way that my suffering has come at my own hand.
>
> Though I have pointed the finger at others, today I wish to confess to You that I have sinned and am responsible not only for the hurt in my life, but in the lives of others also. Please forgive me and cleanse me, as the Bible has promised. Please comfort those who hurt because of my actions and give them a heart of forgiveness toward me. Please help me restore that to which I have brought pain. Jesus, refresh me with Your presence in this time; I seek and need Your help. In Your name I pray, Amen.

It's Never Too Late

Repeatedly, the Bible tells us that we must live by God's standards—not our own standards or "politically correct" standards. If a person repents of his or her sins, then he or she must turn away from those sins. Sometimes, of course, it is difficult to give up that which we have held so dearly for so long. A silly little story makes a fairly good point of this.

A little boy was playing outside in the dirt when it began to lightly rain. His mother called him in for supper, and when she saw him covered with mud, she was very upset. "Upstairs, young man! You get into the bathtub and get clean right now!" The family was seated a few minutes later, waiting for junior to come to the table. Finally, the mother went up to the bathroom to find a shiny clean boy, standing next to a bathtub full of mud and dirt. What a mess. The mother said, "What are you doing, son?" "Oh hi, Mom! I'm just standing here remembering how dirty I was."

That's how it is sometimes with us. We would rather stand still and remember our past than walk forward with God by faith. But that will never bring healing to our souls; in fact, it will always have the opposite effect.

Though you may struggle with confessing what you have done, it is usually much harder to repent. Let me say this: If you want to feel the tender touch of God, then confess your sins and repent from them. God is pleased when we acknowledge what He already knows. He is a holy God, and sin separates us from Him. Confession and repentance help to dress our wound so that the healing process can begin. It is at this point that the poisons in our soul can be purged and we can get back on the road to health.

Come Home!

Millions of people in America had a childhood experience with Jesus, but they have been away from Him so long, in so many different types of sin, that they can't find their way back home. The way home is through confession and repentance. Please come home to Jesus! Please confess your sin and repent! Come back to Jesus and let Him not only stop the painful bleeding that has plagued you, but also let Him dress your wound.

As one person penned:

> If all the sleeping folk will wake up,
> If all the lukewarm folk will fire up,
> If all the dishonest folk will confess up,
> If all the disgruntled folk will cheer up,
> If all the depressed folk will cheer up,
> If all the estranged folk will make up,
> If all the gossipers will shut up,
> If all true soldiers will stand up,
> If all the dry bones will shake up,
> If all the church members will pray up . . .
>   Then we can have a revival![3]

Let today be a fresh, new start in your life. Don't hesitate to cry out to a loving and forgiving God. He is standing by right now, ready to take you into His arms.

11

The Juggernaut of Forgiveness

—The Tender Touch of God—

Doctors tell us that mental disturbances put more people in the hospital than do physical ailments. Perhaps foremost among those mental disturbances is the distress caused by the failure to forgive. Dr. Menninger of the famous Menninger Clinic says that thousands of people could leave their sickbeds if they could just forgive themselves. I read an article recently by a psychologist who said many people come for reconciliation ready to forgive, but not to be forgiven.

Forgiveness—whether of ourselves or of others—is a crucial part of the healing process. Imagine the potential for good if everyone forgave those who had wronged them. Our hospitals would empty out more quickly than if medical science overnight discovered a cure for cancer.

A Prodigal Father

My father died a couple of years ago. He really didn't know me since he and my mother were divorced when I was four years old. I saw him perhaps a dozen times in my life; nine of them were as an adult, and they occurred over a 20-year period. Besides that, there were a few phone calls to check up on him and to help him sell his house and move to a small apartment where he spent his last days. And that's it.

My dad was an alcoholic and a gambler. He was never able to put what was obviously a sharp mind to work for good. He was tall, handsome, deep-voiced, and a real charmer. But in speaking with him hours on end while I tried to catch up on my heritage, I found that our family suffered from a real alcohol problem on his side of the family.

My dad was never allowed to grow up and be a man. His mother refused to "cut the cord." This man would have to be labeled a "mama's boy." When things went badly for him in his adult years, he ran to two places: first to the bottle and second to his mother. She always took him in and protected him from the life that seemed ever so difficult for him.

Nineteen seventy-three was the first time I had seen him in ten years. I was preaching at the Memorial Coliseum in Portland, and I called to see if he wanted to come and meet me. He had the flu, so he invited me to come and see him instead. It was a sad meeting in some ways, but in others it was good. By this time he had become a recluse, living in the converted attic of a big two-story house with a basement—the same house I lived in when I was two years old, the same house his father had built 60 years earlier.

Apparently he never strayed far from home. During our reunion conversation, I sat on the floor of his attic bedroom while he lay in bed. I asked, "Dad, did you ever feel guilty about not being there for me and my brother? Did you ever feel bad that you were never a father to your children? That you never consistently supported us and made our mother suffer so?"

Please don't take me wrong; these questions were not asked in bitterness or spite, but were presented gently. They were questions I had asked a thousand times over in my own head, many of those times in a drunken state in some lonely Portland pool hall or tavern.

His response rings in my ears still today. He began to cry and turned to face the wall. He responded in a manner I never expected, but did hope for. "YES!" he said in a big, resounding voice. "Every day of my life I face the failures I have had. I am a weak man, and the bottle is where I have hidden all these years. I have always felt guilty that I let you boys and your mother down."

My father had been married twice, each marriage producing two boys. Kent and I have two half brothers living in Oregon.

My heart was touched, and I began to tell him of the hurt and pain I had suffered without a father to help guide me. I told him I became a heavy drinker by 20 years of age, fathered an illegitimate baby at 17, then suffered a failed marriage caused largely by drug and alcohol abuse. I described a most miserable life—a life filled with bitterness and anger that sometimes turned into uncontrollable rage.

"You see, Dad, I have been just as big a failure in my own life," I said. "But I have good news to tell you: I have found forgiveness from God. Dad, I forgive you and don't want you ever to feel guilty again." When my father heard me forgive him, he was released from 30 years of pain and guilt.

He replied that he, too, believed in God. Throughout his 50 years of belonging to Alcoholics Anonymous, he knew that a higher power was necessary to maintain sobriety. Though he never could get rid of the bottle—even when he reached his eighties—he tried so desperately to believe. His higher power was a vague force, however, not the personal Friend whom I had described.

More than ten years later, before he died, I was able to visit him again and explain God's great love for him. I told him that even while he was a sinner, Jesus died on the cross for him. I said that God would forgive him of all his past mistakes, failures, and sins. I shared that the blood of Jesus was pure and untainted, and it was that shed blood that God accepted as the sacrifice for Wilbur Hershel MacIntosh. Words can't express the feeling as I stood there in that living room with my arm around my dad, praying with him that the Lord would come into his life and forgive him of his sin.

My dad at last discovered that we are never too old to deal with the pain, the hurt, the memories of old sins. We don't need to keep on reliving the past. We don't need to continue walking through the hurts. God took them all and placed them upon His Son Jesus when He was hanging upon the cross.

Maybe you're like my dad: "Hi, my name is Mack and I'm an alcoholic." You cannot let the past go. Now, in no way am I knocking Alcoholics Anonymous or any of the self-help organizations that have assisted millions of people. Having been where many of these people have been, I can sympathize. But when I found healing for my soul, it wasn't by looking for a higher being; it came by finding God Himself. The same is true for my dad. For all eternity my dad can now say, "Hi, I'm Mack and I'm a child of God." The old has passed away. Everything has become brand-new! And all of it was made possible by forgiveness.

Receiving Forgiveness

Most of us are perhaps willing to forgive—but forget? No way. We keep dragging up old sins and reminding ourselves how bad we are. Often we can forgive others more easily than we can forgive ourselves. I love the brilliant works of C.S. Lewis. In *Letters of C.S. Lewis/Don Giovanni Calabria*, he wrote, "I think that if God forgives us we must forgive ourselves. Otherwise it is almost like setting up ourselves as a higher tribunal than Him."

Howard Hendricks, the gifted Christian communicator, writer, and lecturer from Dallas Theological Seminary, tells of a little boy who asked his mother where he came from, and also where she had come from as a baby. His mother gave him a tall tale about a beautiful white-feathered bird. The boy ran into the next room and asked his grandmother the same question, and received a variation on the bird story.

He then scampered outside to his playmate with the comment, "You know, there hasn't been a normal birth in our family for three generations!"

This helps keep things in perspective. There hasn't been a sinless birth in the human family except for Jesus Christ, and we need to remember that. If our greatest need had been information, God would have sent us an educator. If our greatest need had been technology, God would have sent us a scientist. If our greatest need had been money, God would have sent us an economist. But since our greatest need was forgiveness, God sent us a Savior.

God has shown the epitome of forgiveness by making His Son the required sacrifice for our sins. Have you ever stopped to think that you and I murdered God's only begotten Son? We are guilty. There is no "beyond a reasonable doubt" with God or His heavenly angels. You are guilty. So am I. And that's a fact. Yet when we come to Christ, we are forgiven of all our sins.

You may say that you really are not sure that God will forgive you for the horrible things you have done. Listen, my friend. Just before Jesus Christ died on the cross, He spoke words of forgiveness. He cried out to God, "Father, forgive them, for they do not know what they do" (Luke 23:34). Now, if Jesus could ask God to forgive mankind 2000 years ago as He was dying on a cross for their sins, you had better believe that He will forgive you today.

God gave His Son Jesus for *us*. He came for *us*. He died for *us*. He rose from the dead for *us*. God did this so that you and I would know that He forgave us of all our sins. If you have prayed for the Lord to forgive you, rest assured that God has heard your prayer. He has completely forgiven you and will never bring it up again. He has let it go, so you need to let it go also.

The following Bible verse is one of my favorites, mainly because I am a man who needs lots of forgiveness: "Therefore if any man be in Christ, he is a new creature: old things are passed away; behold, all things are become new" (2 Corinthians 5:17 KJV).

Forgiving Others

The New Testament uses two primary words for forgiveness. One term means "pardon." Another means "to release from bondage or imprisonment." When we are forgiven, not only are we pardoned, we are released from the bondage of sin. Whoever receives such forgiveness is expected to echo it in the way they treat others.

Jesus both taught and lived the message of forgiveness. While instructing His disciples during the early days of His ministry, He gave what is commonly known as "The Sermon on the Mount." Forgiveness was one of the primary themes of His world-famous instruction. Approximately 25 times, Jesus used the word *forgive*. In what we call the Lord's Prayer, He prayed, "and *forgive* us our debts, as we *forgive* our debtors" (Matthew 6:12 KJV).

When we think of debts, we usually think of the Visa or MasterCard bill; debts are money owed to our creditors. But what Jesus has in mind here is much deeper than that. This is an encouragement to have God forgive us as we forgive others. We each owe a great debt to the Lord, and He forgave us. In the same manner, if we have truly been born again, we are required to forgive those who owe us a debt, whatever kind of debt that might be. Jesus makes this point even clearer in Matthew 6:14,15:

> For if you forgive men their trespasses, your heavenly Father will also forgive you. But if you do not forgive men their trespasses, neither will your Father forgive your trespasses.

Again, the principle is "Forgive and be forgiven; refuse to forgive, and neither will God forgive you." That sure puts a huge amount of responsibility on our shoulders, doesn't it? If we want the peace and refreshment that comes with forgiveness, then we need to practice what we preach.

Peter certainly heard all this talk about forgiveness, but he wasn't too sure what it meant. That is why he asked Jesus in Matthew 18:21, "Lord, how often shall my brother sin against me, and I forgive him? Up to seven times?" Now, that sounds like a pretty righteous dude, doesn't it? Peter was willing to forgive somebody seven times.

Jesus' response must have blown Peter's mind. Jesus said to him, "I do not say to you, up to seven times, but up to seventy times seven" (Matthew 18:22). If my math serves me correctly, Jesus is saying that we should be willing to forgive a person *490 times!* As Lucy would say, "Good grief, Charlie Brown!" That's a lot of forgiveness. What Peter had suggested sounded awfully spiritual; he was willing to stretch his forgiveness seven times the norm. Yet the forgiveness Jesus had in mind expanded Peter's expectations by 70-fold (and no doubt was meant to expand them infinitely).

Oh, how great is the love of God! What will it take to teach us forgiveness toward others? One of the best ways, perhaps, is through a story. So now Jesus turns to what He seemed to do best: tell a story. Jesus was the all-time storyteller. The following parable is built on the principle just given:

> Therefore is the kingdom of heaven likened unto a certain king, which would take account of his servants. And when he had begun to reckon, one was brought unto him, which owed him ten thousand talents. But forasmuch as he had not to pay, his lord commanded him to be sold, and his wife, and children, and all that he had, and payment to be made. The servant therefore fell down, and worshipped him, saying, Lord, have patience with me, and I will pay thee all. Then the lord of that servant was moved with compassion, and loosed him, and forgave him the debt.
>
> But the same servant went out, and found one of his fellowservants, which owed him an hundred pence: and he laid hands on him, and took him by the throat, saying, Pay me that thou owest. And his fellowservant fell down at his feet, and

besought him, saying, Have patience with me, and I will pay thee all. And he would not: but went and cast him into prison, till he should pay the debt.

So when his fellowservants saw what was done, they were very sorry, and came and told unto their lord all that was done. Then his lord, after that he had called him, said unto him, O thou wicked servant, I forgave thee all that debt, because thou desiredst me: shouldest not thou also have had compassion on thy fellowservant, even as I had pity on thee? And his lord was wroth, and delivered him to the tormentors, till he should pay all that was due unto him.

So likewise shall my heavenly Father do also unto you, if ye from your hearts forgive not every one his brother their trespasses (Matthew 18:23-35 KJV).

This simple story shows us the fruit of a wound that was never dressed properly. Bitterness kept the man from receiving the forgiveness his master so freely gave to him. Had he accepted the love that came with the forgiveness, he would easily have forgiven those who owed him.

This man's anger seems almost ridiculous. After all the master had done for him, wouldn't you think he would be so grateful and excited that he would be full of thanksgiving? You'd think he would be gracious to his debtor—but he wasn't.

What was his problem? Could it have been pride, revenge, bitterness, or a get-even attitude? We don't know (it was a story, anyway). But we can be sure that those attitudes will destroy some of the most productive years of our life. "Forgive and you shall be forgiven." If you want God's tender touch, then this is the way: Forgive!

Forgiving those who have hurt you is a powerful key to healthy living. Take the key and open the door to your heart and forgive those who have hurt you. A great freedom will come to you. It will be as if the doctor in the emergency room just dressed a deep wound and gave you a prescription designed to relieve the pain. Great calm comes over the heart when a hurt has been dressed.

And what do you have to lose by forgiving? If the people are out of your life, then forgiving them makes no difference to you because you do not have to interact with them. If they are still in your life, then forgive them verbally or even quietly in your heart. It will bring a new dimension to your relationship without you losing a thing—except heartache and pain. And what is heartache and pain worth on the open market today? Nothing!

So face the cross and see forgiveness in full bloom. You will not only give a blessing to others, but you will also receive a blessing in return. The blessing is that the love of God can forgive and heal in your life, too. Failure to forgive clogs the blessing of God.

Two days ago I went with my sons to jump in the spa. We were having trouble getting the heater to work, and again the spa was cold. We just couldn't figure out why the spa was not heating. So I called one of our intern pastors and asked if he would mind stopping by to help me solve the problem. (Before desiring to enter the ministry, this man had been in the pool business.) He did some basic trouble-shooting, then he struck pay dirt. He took out the filter and found that not only had it collected the usual handful of pine needles, leaves, and general debris, it had also picked up a golf ball and one of my sons' T-shirts. This caused the pressure to fall too low to trigger the heater. Once we moved the items from the clogged filter, the heater immediately turned on.

Just like that filter, sometimes our hearts get clogged. We need to realize that the Holy Spirit doesn't flow easily through clogged vessels. The way to remedy the problem is to open your hearts and forgive.

Remember, the pain will always be there unless we dress the wound with forgiveness. Comedian Buddy Hackett says he doesn't bother to carry a grudge. "I've had a few arguments with people, but I never carry a grudge," he says. "You know why? While you're carrying a grudge, they're out dancing."

If we truly are born again, we must learn that forgiveness is a great way to dress the wound. Forgiveness cleanses your soul like a good sorbet cleanses your palate.

The Place of Prayer

Let's suppose that we've accepted the need to forgive. That's one thing; it's quite another to know how to do it. How can we become people of forgiveness? I believe it is in prayer that we find the grace to forgive and the grace to be forgiven. This is the place to find the tender touch of God as we dress our wound with the sweet balm of forgiveness.

When, at the request of the governor of Oklahoma, Billy Graham and his wife, Ruth, joined with their son Franklin to pray for the victims of the Oklahoma City bombing, they found that thousands of people were willing to line up in a cold, stiff wind outside the arena, just to pray. People's emotions were in turmoil. Anger battled with love. Callers swamped Oklahoma City radio talk-shows, some insisting that the perpetrators be shot on sight, while others said prayers must be offered for the bombers' salvation. The desire to forgive rather than seek revenge, expressed by many people in this Bible-belt city, impressed journalists. In fact, an atheist told a local pastor he had never experienced such love.

While Mr. Graham was praying in the arena, all of the federal law-enforcement agents and work crews stopped, took off their hard hats, and bowed their heads for five minutes of silence and prayer in front of and around the building. As I stood there, I sensed a break in the skies over Oklahoma City. It was as if a demonic war was raging over the city, and these prayers broke the power of Satan. I'm convinced your prayers can have the same effect. Prayer and forgiveness go hand-in-hand, and they're a juggernaut of a team.

Forgiveness on Death Row

Sometime ago I was invited to Singapore to hold some meetings. One of the highlights for me was the opportunity to visit the prisons and speak to inmates about Jesus.

My visit began with a ride to the prison in a caravan of cars from the headquarters of the Singapore Department of Prisons. I was told to get into a car with "the minister." As we rode along, it dawned on me that this minister was well-to-do. We were sitting together in the backseat of a Mercedes Benz, a chauffeur driving us to Chang Ghi prison. Out of curiosity I asked him what church he pastored. He said he didn't understand. At that moment I caught the eye of the chauffeur in the mirror; he was laughing, but I didn't know why. When I repeated my question, the minister said he didn't pastor a church.

"But I was led to believe you are a minister," I said.

"Oh! Yes, of course," he replied. "I am the Minister of Labor." "Right! I knew that!" He was a dignitary going to see the services at the prison. After a quick stop at the first prison, we left to visit a second.

It was Christmas, and the superintendent allowed us to visit death row and minister to four or five dozen men. We sang carols and read the Christmas story. The condemned men sat quietly listening while guards stood outside in the hallways. When an invitation to ask God to forgive them of their sins was given, three-fourths of those inmates prayed to receive Jesus into their lives.

I counseled a 19-year-old boy who was going to be hung in two weeks. His crime was murder. He was happy that he had found eternal life, but he told me, "Mike, I know that I am saved from my sin. I know that when I am hung and my neck breaks that I will go to heaven. But still I am mad."

"Why?" I asked.

He admitted that he and some buddies killed three men, but he had been found guilty of killing all three. He said he deserved to hang for killing one man in a drug deal, but he didn't deserve to die for the other two; his buddies had killed them. I told him to forgive his buddies and to spend the next two weeks forgiving himself as well as those who had hurt him. I also suggested he spend the next two weeks reading the Bible and praying. He had so much life and vibrancy, it seemed a shame to see his young life cut off in midstream.

Sometime later I inquired about that young man. Before he was scheduled to be hung, the court found some discrepancies in the trial transcripts and ordered him brought before a judge again. The judge asked if there was anything the young man wanted to say. He replied that he had murdered only one man, not three, and it wasn't fair that he was going to hang in two days for murders he didn't commit.

Then, with the leading of the Holy Spirit, he told the judge that he no longer was angry at the court or bitter with his friends. Jesus Christ had come into his heart two weeks earlier and had forgiven him of all his sins. He told the judge that he had great peace in his heart, and whatever the judge decided was in the hands of God. At that, the judge reread the documents and records in dispute, ruled a mistrial, and dismissed the charges against the man. The last I was told, the young man was so elated and grateful to God that he became an evangelist, went across the border into Malaysia, and is preaching the gospel to the Muslims.

It is time that you, too, feel the tender touch of God. He forgives you, so please forgive yourself. If others have hurt you, forgive them and so receive the blessing of Jesus. Take a tip from an unmarked tombstone outside Sydney, New York. Whoever is buried there learned this lesson well. The tombstone contains but one word of three syllables: *Forgiven.*

12

Basic Equipment

—*The Tender Touch of God*—

No matter where you happened to visit a hospital emergency room, it's likely you would find some of the same vital equipment: antiseptic, syringes, bandages, operating table, surgical knives, special lights, heart monitors, defibrillators, etc. While some hospitals might be better equipped than others, virtually all will have on hand a certain basic set of equipment. Why? Because that equipment is vital to saving lives.

In the same way, no matter what injury might be hurting you right now, there is a basic set of "equipment" that is vital to your recovery and well-being. Whatever your hurt and whatever your pain, there are at least three items that you simply can't do without.

But don't rush down to the medical supply center to pick them up. You won't find them there. The only place to find these three items is within yourself. God places them there, but you're the one who has to use them. These three vital items are courage, patience, and perseverance.

Courage: Little Used, Much Needed

Courage is a little-used word in the vocabulary of today's MTV generation, yet courage is necessary every step of the way on the road to recovery. It takes courage—sometimes, tremendous courage—to face the trials and tribulations of our lives. Too often people turn to self-pity or a negative attitude instead of courage, yet it takes no more effort to choose courage than to opt for one of the available alternatives.

My friend Hal Kuykendall told me a tremendous story of courage and bravery involving his good friend Mike Thornton and Lt. Tommy Norris, both of them Congressional Medal of Honor recipients.

Mike and Tommy were members of a Navy SEAL Platoon that was nearly wiped out in a firefight during the Vietnam War. Mike and Tommy were the only two American Seals in the platoon, the rest were South Vietnamese Seals. This platoon of 14 men ran into a North Vietnamese Army (NVA) company that greatly outnumbered the Seals. During the ensuing fire, Tommy suffered a head wound when a bullet entered his eyes and exited through his temple. Mike was separated from Tommy by approximately 105 yards when the surviving Vietnamese Seals ran to Mike and reported that Tommy had been killed. Refusing to leave Tommy behind, Mike ran back through intense enemy fire, picked up Tommy and carried him a few hundred yards to the beach. The NVA were chasing Mike and firing at him while he was carrying Tommy to the beach. As Mike entered the surf with Tommy, he emptied his M-60 machine gun and then discarded it into the surf and began swimming to sea with the unconscious Tommy in tow. Mike had no idea where he was swimming to, but was hoping he would find a U.S. ship. After swimming a few miles he saw the *USS Newport News* on the horizon. Mike fired a flare into the air and a rescue team from the *USS Newport News* picked up the two battered Seals.

The doctors saved the life of Lt. Tommy Norris, yet not without cost. Mr. Norris had major injuries to his head and he lost one of his eyes.

How self-serving it would have been for Mike Thornton to forget his buddy and put his own safety first. How easy it would have been to look at the wounded Tommy Norris and decide that he could never live through such a devastating injury. Yet Mike was not willing to do that.

I wonder how many Tommy Norris stories are unwritten? How many nameless heroes have mustered the courage to help a fallen comrade? Mike Thornton may think it was natural for him to risk his own life for another, but it was truly a courageous act. And his friend owes his life to Mike's courage.

Sir Ernest Shackleton placed the following advertisement in London newspapers in 1900 in preparation for the National Antarctic Expedition. Later, Sir Shackleton was to say, "It seemed as though all the men in Great Britain were determined to accompany me, the response was so overwhelming."

MEN WANTED
FOR HAZARDOUS JOURNEY.

Small wages, bitter cold, long months of complete darkness, constant danger, safe return doubtful. Honor and recognition in case of success.

This incident suggests that there is some amount of courage in all of us. Even the Cowardly Lion of *Wizard of Oz* fame found he had courage at the moment it was really needed; he just needed a push.

It is likely you need courage right now to face your ordeal, whatever it is. Like the Cowardly Lion, you may doubt that you have any courage. But you do. God placed it within you when the Holy Spirit took up residence inside you. Oh, you may not need the courage of a Navy SEAL, but you do need courage to make that phone call or write that letter or to face an opponent. So call on the courage God has placed within you. Move out in faith, knowing that God is with you all the way. Courage is both a necessary and a beautiful part of your healing. It's one of the chief items God will use to dress your wound.

Thousands of courageous people have gotten back into the swing of things after suffering tremendous hurts. And it seems to me that three recurring factors in their healing process are 1) a strong determination; 2) a personal faith in God—"I can do all things through Christ who strengthens me"; and 3) courage to go beyond the tragedy or pain in their lives.

Perhaps you need the courage to face some physical trial. We all know of courageous people who have overcome tremendous obstacles to regain the use of a limb or even their whole body.

Joni Eareckson Tada is a perfect example of someone who gained victory despite a physical problem. As a teen she dove into a lake, hit the bottom with her head, and broke her neck. She was never able to walk again. Joni has worked hard and courageously to be productive with her life—writing books, painting pictures, and drawing beautiful greeting cards by holding a pen in her teeth. If that were not enough, she has recorded music, spoken out on behalf of handicapped people, and shared her Christian faith around the world with millions of people. Through an organization she began called Joni and Friends, she has helped thousands of people with disabilities to find courage to go on with their lives.

Or consider the story of Dennis Byrd, a former professional football player who gained success, riches, and popularity. Add a beautiful wife, and what more could a man ask for? Little did he expect that in one play his career would end, leaving him with a broken neck and paralysis. Yet against tremendous odds, Dennis made a miraculous recovery. With strong determination and his personal faith in God, he began a strenuous physical rehabilitation program that has been remarkably successful. He is an inspiration not only to New York Jets fans, but to people everywhere.

Of course, courage doesn't show up only in volunteers for dangerous expeditions to the unknown. Courage doesn't appear only in heroic combat situations. Courage isn't needed only to overcome physical disabilities. Courage is exercised every day by people just like you and me, even though it may not be recognized as front-page news. Just because the president of the United States doesn't present you with a Congressional Medal of Honor doesn't mean that you have exercised no courage. It takes courage to be honest. It takes courage to be faithful.

An attractive young woman whose career required a good deal of travel was asked if she was ever bothered by uninvited male attention. She answered, "Never. I just say five words and immediately I am left alone." And what are those five words? "I simply ask, 'Are you a born-again Christian?'"

For this young woman, such a response is courageous. Although it may not be the kind of heroism needed for a secret military operation, nevertheless it demonstrates real courage. God is pleased with it, and it enables her to overcome hurtful situations that might well overwhelm others.

Patience

We are the children of the "buy now, pay later" and "you deserve a break today" generation. We have drive-through restaurants, one-hour dry cleaners, 24-hour ATM machines, instant car washes, and ten-minute lube and oil changes. We have speedy check-in services for our car rentals, 30-minute home delivery pizza, and we can even order stamps by mail. Everyone is in such a hurry. We're so busy being busy that we have no time to stop and smell the flowers.

Patience is another priceless virtue we seem terribly short on. Yet life requires patience—sometimes truckloads of the stuff. Johann Wolfgang von Goethe penned:

> We must not hope to be mowers,
>> And to gather the ripe gold ears,
> Unless we have first been sowers
>> And watered the furrows with tears.
>
> It is not just as we take it,
>> This mystical world of ours,
> Life's field will yield as we make it
>> A harvest of thorns or of flowers.

Patience is crucial in receiving the tender touch of God. In His timing, all things will work out for the best.

I admit that patience is not my forte. It has taken the Lord 26 years of trials and tribulations to help me become more patient. I am much like the woman whom

William Yates, pastor of the Baptist church in Pfafftown, North Carolina, describes.

In the small town where the Reverened Yates grew up, it was the policeman's job to answer the volunteer fire department's telephone and then to sound the fire whistle to rally the volunteers to duty. One Saturday morning his father, the chief of police, had just come on duty when the fire department phone rang. When he answered it, a voice on the other end of the line frantically said, "Send the fire truck!" Then the caller immediately slammed the phone down.

His dad stood stunned, not knowing what to do. In a few minutes the phone rang again. Quickly, he picked it up and said again, "Fire Department." Again the voice cried, "Send the fire truck!" And again the caller immediately hung up.

Realizing that someone's house was possibly at stake, he rushed outside and scanned the sky to see if he could see smoke and therefore send the fire trucks in that direction. While outside he also devised a plan about how to keep the caller from hanging up so quickly if she called back. Sure enough, the phone rang again and he went running inside. Picking up the phone, he said, "Where's the fire?" The lady on the other end screamed, "In the kitchen!" and slammed the phone down again.

I identify with this story a lot. Sometimes impatience can cause us and others much harm. We need to realize that sometimes God chooses to heal us over time, not in an instant. I have discovered that my own back injury fits into this category. The Lord has been gracious to me in revealing the nature of the injury, as well as a plan for healing it. Yet that plan requires time to bring me its full benefit. If I grow impatient and try to shortcut the plan or jettison it entirely, my back will grow worse than it was before. So I must be patient and partner with God in my healing.

Unfortunately, too many in this fast-paced society of ours are filled with an obsession with the immediate and have little interest in the long-term. This often is illustrated to me as a pastor. Many church people don't want the disciplines of Jesus. They want the fun without the commitment. To some people, the church is like a smorgasbord. They choose and pick what they want, running to the dessert table while leaving out the vegetables and meat. When it comes to prayer meetings, tithing, or a Bible-study group, they lose interest. If it is easy, fun, and promises immediate gratification, they may show up.

Such an attitude prevents the cultivation of patience. Remember, it was Jesus who said, "If you abide in My word, you are My disciples indeed" (John 8:31). The fruit of a disciple is that he or she is reading, studying, and loving the words of Jesus, and above all doing his or her best to live them out in everyday practice. It takes patience to grow in the knowledge and grace of God.

We need to slow down a bit and not take ourselves so seriously. We need to get hold of the eternal. We don't even think of the concept of eternity very often. Eternity is forever and ever. We think in terms of the now or today or tomorrow. We forget that time is longer than our short few years on this planet. Scripture teaches us that our life is "even a vapor that appears for a little time and then vanishes away" (James 4:14). We are tempted to lose courage and lose patience because of our troubles, yet all the while God is silently working.

My friend, there is hope, there is a way out of this mess you are in. There is someone who cares, and there is an answer. Impatient living for the things of this world is not how you want to continue. These things are going to vanish. Eternal living is going to give you a purpose for tomorrow's sunrise. Eternal principles give a reason to get out of bed and to get going.

Impatience and an unwillingness to trust God to do the right thing in His time leads to loss of perspective. Dr. Jack Kevorkian, dubbed "Dr. Death" by the media, deals in the temporal. When patients with terminal illnesses come to him, he has only a temporal solution. He sells death as the only way out of these heartbreaking physical dilemmas. Yet suicide and immediate death is not the only answer. Jesus Christ, the Author and Finisher of our faith, has a message of hope to dispense, a message of eternal value. Think of the miracles that might happen in the lives of distraught patients if they were given hope. Even if their bodies died, still they would live (see John 11:25,26). They would spend their last moments on this earth glorying in the truth of Romans 8:18: "For I consider that the sufferings of this present time are not worthy to be compared with the glory which shall be revealed in us."

Yet I do not condemn those who make temporal living their priority. I understand how their thinking has been shaped by the pressures of society and the molding of a humanistic education system and a culture whose foundation is based on the love of money. I do not condemn them, but I do try to show them a better way. The way of Jesus. The way of the cross. The way of trust in and dependence upon a loving God who does all things well in His time.

I love the "Peanuts" cartoon strip written by Charles Schultz. In one strip, when little Sally was still a toddler, Linus and Lucy were watching her crawl by, and Linus asked, "How long do you think it will be before Sally starts to walk?" Lucy replied, "Good grief! What's the hurry? Let her crawl around for a while! Don't rush her! She's got all the time in the world. Once you stand up and start to walk, you're committed for life."

As James taught in his epistle, we must be patient:

> My brethren, count it all joy when ye fall into divers temptations; knowing this, that the trying of your faith worketh patience. But let patience have her perfect work, that ye may be perfect and entire, wanting nothing (James 1:2-4 KJV).

I have learned that patience is a fruit of the Holy Spirit. That means we can call upon God to help us gain patience.

But I warn you: Don't expect to receive it overnight!

Sticking with It

Closely allied to both courage and patience is a third virtue we don't see nearly enough of these days: perseverance. It is perseverance that enables you to keep on going when you would rather quit. It's perseverance that gives you the strength to overcome daunting obstacles in order to accomplish a desirable goal. And it's perseverance that helps you get up off the floor—perhaps for the second or third or even six-hundredth time after being knocked down—and continue on to the end.

Perseverance often means rejecting others' rejection of you. Many of those who have risen from failure to real achievement have rejected the rejection of this world.

In 1902, the poetry editor of *The Atlantic Monthly* returned a sheaf of poems to a 28-year-old poet with this curt note: "Our magazine has no room for your vigorous verse." The poet was Robert Frost, who rejected the rejection.

In 1905, the University of Bern turned down a Ph.D. dissertation as irrelevant and fanciful. The young physics student who wrote the dissertation was Albert Einstein, who rejected the rejection.

In 1894, a rhetoric teacher at Harrow in England wrote on a 16-year-old student's report card: "a conspicuous lack of success." The 16-year-old was Winston Churchill, who rejected the rejection.

It is amazing to note the long list among those who have overcome adversity: Beethoven, whose best works were composed after he had lost his hearing; Louis Pasteur, whose greatest discoveries were made after he had suffered a life-threatening stroke; John Milton, whose best poetry came after he was blind; William Cowper, who wrote his greatest hymns in lucid moments between fits of insanity.

Perseverance allows us to make it through a difficult situation. When courage and patience have done their work, they lead to perseverance. I know how difficult life can be. I know how easy it is to start thinking that things will never change or get better. I know that giving up is easy and perseverance is difficult. Yet I have found that perseverance is not only a great character builder, but that it also leads to rewards that can be won in no other way.

When the United States pulled out of Vietnam at the close of the war there, a tremendous exodus occurred of people who did not want to live under Communist rule. These desperate people clamored for hope and a future, both for themselves and their children. Thousands of these people were allowed to relocate to the United States. Camp Pendelton Marine Base in San Diego County was used to process these new immigrants. Years ago I went to the base to try and help relocate many of these dear people.

Since then, I have been amazed at how well the Vietnamese community has assimilated itself into the American lifestyle. Through hard work and perseverance, two thirds of these people have found jobs, and many of their children are pulling straight A's in American schools. These are boat people, survivors of a journey that many people didn't survive. They would never have made it without large doses of perseverance.

Steve Palermo is another man who knows firsthand the rewards of perseverance. Do you remember his tragic story? Steve was shot in the back on July 6, 1991, while coming to the aid of a robbery victim in the parking lot of a Dallas restaurant. Because of his wounds, Steve lost partial use of his legs.

Before the shooting, Steve was a successful American League umpire. Steve loved his job. He joined the American League umpiring staff in 1977 when he was 27 years old. He worked one World Series, four League Championship Series and the 1986 All-Star Game. He was a success in his field and was admired and appreciated by his peers.

Moments after the bullet entered his body, all that was gone. Nothing but a memory. What would you have done? How would you have responded? Steve could have let this tragedy warp his personality, filling him with self-pity and bitterness. Instead, Steve worked hundreds of hours at rehabilitating himself and has made tremendous progress.

In fact, not long ago Steve was named special assistant to the chairman of major league baseball's governing council. Today, with the help of crutches, Steve walks and stands and makes a big contribution to the game he still loves.[1]

It never would have happened without courage, patience, and above all, perseverance. Steve took immediate steps to dress his wound, and his life is a compelling example of what such determined action can accomplish.

What about you? How are you responding to the hurt and pain in your own life? Are you tempted to give up? To give in to bitterness and defeat? To harbor the pain instead of dressing the wound? I beg you, don't. Now, more than ever, you need to ask God for an extra portion of courage, patience, and perseverance. With His help and the assistance of friends, you can make it through this difficult time. You can emerge stronger at the other end of the tunnel. Whatever you do, don't give up. Life can be sweet once more. As the writer of Hebrews reminds us:

> Therefore do not cast away your confidence, which has great reward. For you have need of endurance, so that after you have done the will of God, you may receive the promise: "For yet a little while, and He who is coming will come and will not tarry" (Hebrews 10:35-37).

Life Is Difficult, Not Impossible

Life is difficult, but it is never impossible. To make it through life's rough spots, we need courage, patience, and perseverance. It may not be easy. It may not be painless. It may not be quick. But God *will* honor your steps of faith. Don't rush things. Remember, God is silently working on your behalf.

The pain of our situations may almost drive us to call the Dr. Kevorkians of this world, but we know today we will never make such a call. God's tender touch will reach us. God is working silently on our behalf. The devil will try to make us curse God. He will try to drive away godly reasoning. He will try to keep us from dressing the wound. He will try to keep us from the Bible and prayer. But we don't have to give in. God has limitless supplies of courage, patience, and perseverance in His divine storehouses. But it's up to us to ask for them and to put them to use.

The Lord instructs us in Psalms, "Call upon Me in the day of trouble; I will deliver you, and you shall glorify Me" (Psalm 50:15). All the help you need is available to you. Right now. Maybe you don't have a history of following through. Perhaps you don't know how to reject the rejection. Jesus will help you. Won't you give Him a chance?

PART THREE
Let God Heal

The Tender Touch of God

13

A Waterfall of Liquid Love

The Tender Touch of God

If you ever get the chance to visit the beautiful state of Oregon, you must visit the Columbia River Gorge. It truly is one of God's great masterpieces—a miniature Grand Canyon with the mighty Columbia River winding through it, separating the state of Washington on its north shore and the state of Oregon on its south shore. It is a must-see, lying less than a one-hour drive from the Portland International Airport. One of my favorite spots on the planet is found along the scenic highway that follows the gorge. Ever since I was a boy growing up in Portland, one particular spot on this drive has held a special place in my heart.

Multnomah Falls drops over 600 feet to a beautiful pool of water, then flows from that pool to cascade down yet another drop into a second pool, then moves on to the Columbia River. A concrete walking bridge built during the 1930s allows you to hike a trail to the top of the falls and explore Larch Mountain. If you step carefully over the side railing and walk down to the edge of the pool, you will see that centuries of cascading water have carved out a huge cave. You can walk into that grotto and kneel down directly behind the waterfall as it hits the pool. In the summertime it is the most refreshing experience on the planet. The mist and spray blow back into the cave and touch your face. The spray is so soft that it is as if the tender touch of God has caressed you.

Whenever my travels take me to Portland, I always visit Multnomah Falls. It is breathtaking, invigorating, and for me it is spiritually uplifting.

A couple of years ago Bob Hawkins Sr., the founder of Harvest House Publishers, let me and my three sons stay in his company's condominium on the Oregon coast. It was a great trip. We explored the coast, drove dune buggies along the sand dunes at the beach, then took off north to visit other coastal towns. Eventually we left for Portland to see my old stomping grounds and where I attended elementary and high schools. Last I took my sons to Multnomah Falls. We entered the cave, and I let them experience the beauty of God's creation there.

A few months ago my son Jonathan gave me a gift from Nashville where he attends college. When I opened the package, I smiled. Somehow he had found a mounted black-and-white photograph of Multnomah Falls. The shot was taken from the parking lot looking up to the magnificent cascade of fresh, melted snow. Three days ago as I took a break from typing, I went for a walk and stopped in an art gallery. There in front of me was a beautiful color photograph of Multnomah Falls from a different angle.

Now I own two shots of one of my favorite places on earth.

A Northwest Travelogue?

By now you may be asking yourself, "Why are you telling us all this, Mike? Are we on a travel tour of the Northwest?" No, we are not. But I wanted to put a physical picture in your mind that can illustrate a spiritual truth. Multnomah Falls reminds me of God's infinite love. In fact, the night I gave my heart to Jesus it was as if I were standing under a waterfall of pure, liquid love. God's love to me was like standing beneath Multnomah Falls and letting His liquid love overpower my soul, healing long years of hurts.

When I first found out about God's love for me, I was simply overwhelmed. I just could not bring myself to grasp the depth of it. God loves me? *Me?* Why would God love me?

Then it all happened at once. I had asked for prayer and, as the minister laid his hand upon my head and asked God to heal me of all my pain and suffering and to fill me with the Holy Spirit, "Multnomah Falls" poured out upon me. Time stopped; I stopped; thoughts stopped; the world stopped. God began filling me and filling me with love. I was a finite vessel taking in the infinite love of God, and His love began to overflow from me. Twenty-six years later that love is still propelling me to love God and to love people.

God's love was real and is real. And that love heals better than any medicine which science has ever concocted.

A Unique Word

Did you know that the word *love* is one of the most unique words in the world? When the New Testament was written, ancient Greek used a number of words to describe different kinds of love. That makes good sense. How could you compare the love of surfing to the love a man has for a woman? Or how about the love a mother has for her newborn with the love she has for a new chariot?

Two words in ancient Greek were especially popular for describing different kinds of love. Yet these two words were not powerful enough to express God's love to mankind. Therefore the writers of the New Testament took a little-used word and infused it with new meaning. That is why we find three words in the Greek New Testament which are used over and over to express the idea of love.

The word *phileo* basically means "to treat affectionately or kindly, to welcome a friend." The city of Philadelphia—meaning brotherly love—gets its name from this word.

The second most common word was *eros*. We get our English word *erotic* from this term. This word described physical, sensual attraction. Yet neither of these words, of course, adequately expressed the deep love of God in sending His Son to die for us.

Therefore the writers of the New Testament used the term *agape* to describe this greater love. *Agape* describes a profound kind of love, a giving love, a sacrificial love, a selfless love. This kind of love is long-suffering, kind, not envious, not proud, not self-exalting, doesn't misbehave, is not self-seeking, is not easily provoked, doesn't rejoice in evil, does rejoice in the truth, bears all things, believes all things, hopes all things, endures all things, and never fails. When *agape* is at work in our lives, it brings forth joy, peace, long-suffering, gentleness, goodness, faith, meekness, self-control. That's an enormous number of descriptive words to describe this love—but it's also an enormous challenge to daily experience to express this love.

It is this deep, rich, divine love that God uses to heal our hurts. This is the love that comes with the tender touch of God—a love so beautiful, so refreshing, so peaceful, yet so powerful that it can be likened to standing directly beneath Multnomah Falls on a hot summer day. It is a love so deep, so profound that it truly can cover a multitude of sins.

Maybe it has been years since you have given or received love. That in itself will seriously hurt anyone. Whatever your circumstances, this is the day to call upon God to fill you to overflowing with His *agape* love. This is the day to let the tender touch of God begin your healing process.

Let the dam break, the floodwaters overflow—and be healed today by the power of God's *agape* love. It is so divine, so fufilling, so beautiful, so overwhelming, so real. This love of God shows not only His care and deep concern for you, but it shows you His personality as well. The apostle John instructed us that God *is* love. Read the following passage and rejoice that you are loved by the almighty source of love:

> Beloved, let us love one another: for love is of God; and every one that loveth is born of God, and knoweth God. He that loveth not knoweth not God; for God is love. In this was manifested the love of God toward us, because that God sent his only begotten Son into the world, that we might live through him. Herein is love, not that we loved God, but that he loved us, and sent his Son to be the propitiation for our sins.
>
> Beloved, if God so loved us, we ought also to love one another. No man has seen God at any time. If we love one another, God dwelleth in us, and his love is perfected in us. Hereby know we

that we dwell in him, and he in us, because he hath given us of his Spirit. And we have seen and do testify that the Father sent the Son to be the Saviour of the world. Whosoever shall confess that Jesus is the Son of God, God dwelleth in him, and he in God. And we have known and believed the love that God hath to us. God is love; and he that dwelleth in love dwelleth in God, and God in him. Herein is our love made perfect, that we may have boldness in the day of judgment: because as he is, so are we in this world.

There is no fear in love; but perfect love casteth out fear: because fear hath torment. He that feareth is not made perfect in love. We love him, because he first loved us. If a man say, I love God, and hateth his brother, he is a liar: for he that loveth not his brother whom he hath seen, how can he love God whom he hath not seen? And this commandment have we from him, That he who loveth God love his brother also (1 John 4:7-21 KJV).

Note that in these short 15 verses, the word *love* is used 26 times. God is love, and He loved you before you ever loved Him. In fact, He loved you even before you knew He was there! Of course, you can accept or reject that love; it's your prerogative. But know that He loves you and is committed to sharing His love with you.

The Insanity of Life Without God's Love

Life is insane without God's love. Without His love present in and through us, we have no hope.

A story from World War I illustrates how insane life can become. On one side, trenches were filled with Germans; on the other, with Americans. Between the two forces lay a desolate and narrow no-man's-land.

A young German soldier attempting to cross that no-man's-land was shot and had become entangled in the barbed wire. He cried out in great anguish, whimpering periodically. Between explosions, all the Americans could hear the man scream in pain. When one American soldier could stand it no longer, he left his trench and crawled on his belly to the enemy soldier. When the American side realized what their comrade was doing, they stopped firing. Soon a German officer realized what was happening and ordered his own men to cease fire. Now a weird silence enveloped the no-man's-land.

At last the American stood up with the German in his arms, walked straight to the enemy trenches, and placed the wounded soldier in the waiting arms of his comrades. Then the American turned and started back across no-man's-land. Suddenly a hand on his shoulder spun him around. There stood a German officer who wore the Iron Cross, the highest German honor for bravery. He jerked it from his own uniform and pinned it on the American, who walked back to the American trenches. When the soldier reached safety, the insanity of war resumed.

How often we do the same thing. We find ourselves in the midst of trouble, when suddenly we get some kind of reprieve. We feel as if things are going to be okay for a moment; the battle subsides, and we proceed to do what is right. Then, in the blink of an eye, we return to the insanity. We go back into the battle without God's love buoying up our souls.

Hardship and heartbreak cause many people to believe they have no reason to go on living. Things get so bad that they imagine the only way out is to take their own lives. But suicide is never the way to stop the bleeding, to stop the hurt and suffering. Suicide only reminds us that the victim has lost sight of the love of God.

In the past five to ten years, teenagers around the world have committed more suicides than ever before in history. American teenagers appear to be leading the pack. These despairing young people have lost all hope. And in some ways, it's no wonder. If their movies, schools, television programs, and families don't reinforce that there is a happy future available to them, then why go on living? All day long they are exposed to violence in music, violence on television, violence at home, violence on the big screen, violence in the classroom, violence on the street. Where is the hope? Is there a way out of this mess? Yes! It's God's love. That's the answer; it's that simple. If you want to be healed, you must allow God's love to intercede.

Love and Joy

God wants to heal your hurts by imparting love and joy. Love and joy are two tremendous powers which come from God. Both of these powers are a profound presence, reaching into the deepest, darkest area of your soul to turn on the healing lamp of God. Joy flows from the well of love.

When we feel God's tender touch, we experience God's love toward us and for us. That brings joy unspeakable. God's love can easily heal us today because it was faithful yesterday and already has made provision for tomorrow. As the apostle Paul noted,

> Eye hath not seen, nor ear heard, neither have entered into the heart of man, the things which God hath prepared for them that love him (1 Corinthians 2:9 KJV).

God has prepared something for you that is literally out of this world. There is nothing that can keep you from it—unless it is you yourself. This love and joy is tremendous, and it's yours for the receiving:

In all these things we are more than conquerors through him that loved us. For I am persuaded, that neither death, nor life, nor angels, nor principalities, nor powers, nor things present, nor things to come, nor height, nor depth, nor any other creature, shall be able to separate us from the love of God, which is in Christ Jesus our Lord (Romans 8:37-39 KJV).

A vast amount of our hurts come from the lack of love and joy. But just mix these two elements into our recipe of living, and there isn't much in the area of hurt, pain, and suffering that can linger too long. The fact is, the joy of God *heals*.

I know this may sound too simplistic, too easy. Most of us, in our more cynical moments, have questioned the sincerity of those who tell others to "have a nice day." One lady was overheard saying to someone who told her to have a nice day, "I have other plans."

May I ask, What are your plans? Are you ready to take your hurts to God and allow Him to heal you? I urge you to take charge of your life today and begin the process that God has so clearly and carefully presented. He will do all that is necessary if you are simply ready and willing. God will make you able. He loves you so much. He has been in love with you for years. He's seen your smiles and He's seen your tears. Give Jesus a chance. Let God heal you of your hurts. He's ready to do it, you know! His love has the wonderful power to cleanse you today.

Jesus, the Man of Joy

How sad to see this world running in circles, looking in all the wrong places for joy and happiness and love. Jesus, as Dr. Sherwood Wirt says in his recent book, is a man of joy. Although Renaissance painters portray the

Savior as a sad, pathetic, emaciated, scrawny-looking little man—without strength or manhood or other masculine attributes that would appeal to the masses—the Scriptures certainly don't picture Him that way. That's not the Jesus I believe in and love so dearly.

Yes, He was a man of sorrows, and we cannot overlook that aspect of His character. He was brutally tortured before crucifixion took His life from Him. But let us never forget that it was with a "loud voice" that Jesus shouted out His last words on the cross. It was a strong, assertive voice that reminds us God was completely in control on Calvary. Jesus was not a wimp, but a strong and powerful figure who paid the full price for our sins. He was a man pouring out His love to those who killed Him.

The joy of the Lord is so evident in the Gospel accounts. Joy was at the tomb of the resurrected Lazarus, overshadowing the sadness and disappointment of the dead man's sisters. Joy was there when the leper returned to thank Jesus. Joy was there when a woman caught in the very act of adultery was forgiven and released from her sin. Joy was there when the deaf heard, the blind saw, and the lame walked. Joy was there on the mountain sides as the multitudes listened to the profound teachings of Jesus. Joy was there when the little children flocked to Jesus. Joy was there when the boy gave Jesus his lunch so that He could work a miracle and feed the thousands.

Joy was there when Jesus forgave Zaccheus for abusing his authority. Joy was there when Jesus stood up in the boat and stopped the storm. Joy was there that first day of the week when dawn broke and the women knew that Jesus had resurrected from the dead. They ran with "great fear and joy" to tell the disciples. Everywhere Jesus went, joy tagged along.

Often our hurts keep us from the joy of living. We so often forget the good times that our families have had. We forget how we have been through rough times before and yet made it. Phil Dunagan once said, "The Holy Spirit is often compared to a flame or a fire. Paul told Timothy to stir up the gift of God. The Greek word for 'stir up' means to 'rekindle.'"

Now, that requires some personal effort. One of the surest ways to rekindle the Spirit is to take the "poker" of your memory and stir up some past occurrences in your life. Recall the times that God has intervened in your life and answered your prayers. Meditate upon your blessings. Throw the "logs" of praise, thankfulness, and gratitude on the fire of God and just see if the flame of the Holy Spirit does not burn more brightly than ever before.

It is wonderful to see God's joy. That, along with His love, is what caught my attention, drew me to Him, and caused me to surrender my life to Him 26 years ago. It's that unspoken joy of living, that effervescent joy of seeing Him, that can take us through the hurts and painful experiences of life.

Let the joy of the Lord fill your heart today. You have seen that you must stop the bleeding and dress the wound; once that is accomplished, you must rest in God's love and let God heal your hurts.

The Rock That Never Changes

In 1995 something terrible happened in Oregon. I received a copy of a front page of the *Oregonian*, the state's largest newspaper, which featured a horrifying color photograph paired with a distressing article. The article described how a huge boulder weighing several tons had fallen off of the side of Larch Mountain and crashed hundreds of feet below—directly into the pool at Multnomah Falls. The boulder hit the beautiful pond with such force that it sent a spray of sharp rocks and gallons of water over the top of the bridge where a wedding party was taking photos.

Sadly, pedestrians are no longer allowed to walk the small path from the bridge to the grotto. Authorities no longer permit visitors to feel the lovely spray upon their faces from inside the cave. No longer will I be allowed to visit my favorite spot, where time stopped and let me be a kid again. "No Trespassing," the sign says. How sad that future generations will never know what they could have seen and experienced. I grieve that Multnomah Falls, one of my favorite places on earth, has changed.

Yet I remember that the spiritual reality it reminds me of never changes. Multnomah Falls may lose some of its magic through the ravages of erosion, but God's love never erodes, never dims, never diminishes, never stops. God will never put up a "No Trespassing" sign on His love. In fact, the only sign I've ever seen there is written in big, bold, block letters in heaven's eternal ink: COME ON IN! THE WATER'S FINE!

Or as the psalmist said, *"Taste and see that the LORD is good!"* (Psalm 34:8).

14

In His Time

—The Tender Touch of God—

For years Donna Arlow was a faithful Sunday school teacher. During the week she attended college in San Diego, and when she finally graduated, she went on to law school at the University of San Diego. When Donna passed the bar exam, she moved home with her parents to Huntington Beach, about an hour-and-a-half drive to San Diego.

Despite the distance, every Sunday morning she would be on the road by 6 A.M. so she could arrive at church in time to teach her children's Sunday school class, spend the afternoon with friends, attend the evening Bible study, then take another hour and a half to drive home. The next day she would get up at 4 A.M., get dressed, and drive approximately one hour to Beverly

Hills, where she worked with a firm on Wilshire Boulevard. As "low person on the totem pole," Donna arrived early to beat the Los Angeles traffic jams. (Reports last year said the average speed on Los Angeles freeways was 35 MPH and after the turn of the century would be 19 MPH.) Donna was usually the first one to arrive each day. Twenty-nine lawyers worked for this firm, as well as all the others who make a large law firm run.

Donna started each day quietly in her small office with a daily Bible devotion, something her boss always noticed. He was one of three partners who owned this very successful firm on the top floor of a bank building. After several months of this daily routine, Donna and her boss became better acquainted, and she began telling him about Jesus. Donna and other friends living in the Beverly Hills area wanted to begin a midweek Bible study, so I volunteered to do one on Tuesday nights for about 30-40 people each week.

It was during this time that Donna's boss, Paul Engstrom, gave his life to the Lord. A year later I performed their wedding ceremony.

One day Donna called and asked if I would mind going to the hospital to visit a very old and dear friend of her family. Her mother and father, both immigrants from Ireland, had known this woman and her husband when they all arrived together many years before. The woman was in the hospital, dying of cancer, and wasn't given many days to live.

I called Donna's delightful mother and father to get some background on this woman. They loved her dearly; she was like family to them. Their main concern was the woman's soul. They doubted she had ever been born again. What they wanted most of all was for her to hear the gospel of Jesus Christ.

They called their friend and told her that I would be coming by to see her. When I arrived, I was greeted by her whole family. From what I could gather, they were told she could live maybe two days more. Since I had never met the woman or her children or grandchildren, I felt a little awkward. When I introduced myself to the family, they all began to leave the room. I asked them to please stay and said I would come back later, but one of her daughters took me aside and said it was important for me to be there and to have a deep talk with their mother.

After 15 or 20 minutes of "bridge building," I felt it was time to bring up the subject of God. Knowing that she had gone without Him her whole life, I wanted to be especially sensitive to her needs. She was a lovely woman with a delightful personality and truckloads of elegant charm. She was the type who made you feel as if you had been friends forever.

I said that while I didn't mean to embarrass her or make her uncomfortable, I needed to change the subject. I stumbled over my words and then finally said, "Your friends, the Arlows, are very concerned about your soul. So I would like to talk with you about God and heaven."

"Oh!" she exclaimed with tremendous enthusiasm through a face that lit up. "You mean about being born again and repenting of my sins and asking Jesus Christ to come into my heart to be my Lord and Savior?"

Flabbergasted, I took a double take and said, "Why, yes. That's exactly what I'd like to talk to you about."

With a smile that could melt an iceberg she said, "Don't worry about me, Michael. Last week a cute little candy striper came in to see me every day, and she would tell me that Jesus loved me. Then she sat down with me and explained everything and asked me if I wanted to be born again. I said yes, most certainly; what must I do?

And this sweet little thing took my hand and prayed with me, and I asked Jesus to come into my heart. I have been so happy ever since. But I do have one question."

"What is that?" I inquired.

Her response rings in my mind tonight as I type away: "Why didn't I do it sooner? Our family would have been so happy with Jesus."

God had been working all along. For whatever reason, He was waiting for a teenage volunteer to share her faith with this dear lady. Who knows who this young woman is or where she is? God does, and that's what counts. She had done my work for me before I ever arrived. This young woman probably has led many people to the Lord, and this dear lady helped build her confidence with other terminally ill patients.

Imagine—she may stand beside your hospital bed someday and pray with *you*. God also wanted to continue building the friendship between Donna, Paul, her parents, and myself through this experience.

God sees far more of the puzzle than you or I ever could. It is good for us to learn that God is healing when, where, who, why, and how He wants. He is at work healing our hurts, even when we think He has forgotten all about us.

A Long-Lost Baby

The summer following my brother's death, I started dating my next-door neighbor, who was two years older than I was. Little did either of us ever expect that one year later we would be having a baby. Nineteen sixty-one was not like the nineties where unwed teen pregnancies are prevalent. It was a shame for the girl and an embarrassment for both families. We were separated by our parents, and the baby was given up for adoption at birth. I never even knew if it was a boy or a girl.

No one could imagine the guilt and sorrow I felt. It was painful to realize that I was a father and that I was responsible for getting my girlfriend pregnant. I used to stand by our second-story apartment window, staring out and crying. My brother Kent would console me and encourage me that everything would turn out okay.

My teenage pain went deep, very deep. I had hurt one person's life, embarrassed her in front of her family and friends. I had hurt my mother and brother and brought a baby into the world whom I could never see. I knew the deep hurt and anger of the mother's parents, yet there was nothing that could be done.

As we've said throughout this book, pain can cripple us if we let it. Well, I let it. I entered my senior year of high school so full of guilt, sorrow, and emotional turmoil that I dropped out.

But that's not where the story ends. In 1992 God healed me of that 31-year-old hurt in a remarkable way. In His timing, for His glory and our good, He played out for me the incredible truth of "Romans 8:28 (KJV)—"And we know that all things work together for good to them that love God, to them who are the called according to his purpose." Here's how it happened.

Greg Laurie and I have been friends for 24 years. Today Greg pastors a congregation of 10,000-plus, speaks on the popular national radio broadcast "New Beginnings," and is an accomplished evangelist with Harvest Crusades, which has brought hundreds of thousands of people to the Lord.

God had a wonderful plan for the evening of Greg's first Harvest Crusade at the Orange County Fairgrounds Amphitheater. Not only was this evening going to see hundreds enter God's kingdom, but the Lord was going to bring two members of His kingdom together. Franklin Graham, Dennis Agajanian, and Greg were all standing backstage together, talking. I was standing to Greg's left. I turned to greet Tom Gazi, a good friend who works as a Newport Beach police officer. Tom was handling security that evening.

When I turned back to my right, Greg was gone and Karen Johnson was standing in his place. Karen is the wife of Jeff Johnson, the pastor of Calvary Chapel in Downey, California. Karen began and oversees a ministry in the church called The House of Ruth. This work helps women with unwanted pregnancies to take a different road than abortion. Its volunteers love the women through their ordeal and provide them with housing, medical, emotional, and financial support.

The House of Ruth also makes all the necessary arrangements for the legal adoption of the babies. Potential adoptive parents are given an extremely thorough background check, so the birth mother is assured that her child will be placed in a good Christian home. Although it had been three decades since I lost contact with my first child, for some reason I asked Karen, "Do you think you could find a baby who was born in 1961?" She asked if I knew any details concerning the birth, such as the mother's name, date of birth, driver's license number, Social Security number, phone number, address. I knew nothing at all except the mother's name. Next she asked for the name of the hospital. I had no idea, only that it was somewhere in the San Francisco Bay area.

That's not much to go on. If we consider San Mateo, Contra Costa, Marin, Alameda, Santa Clara, and San Francisco counties, we are talking about an area of 3765 square miles. That's a big chunk of land to search in order to find a missing baby who would be 30 years old by now. Those five counties were home to some 5,302,797 people. That's quite a haystack hiding one little needle, isn't it?

Then she asked if I knew the name or location of the doctor who delivered the baby. Now, in 1992 there were 19,318 physicians in these five Bay area counties. What would be the odds that the doctor of 1961 would still be in the Bay area, let alone the state of California? What were the odds that he was around at all? He must be at least 130 years old by now. Karen took down what little information I had, said she would do what she could, and promised to get in contact if she found anything out.

When I returned home I told Sandy about this strange occurrence. Before my encounter with Karen, it hadn't occurred to me to look for this child. Even as Karen educated me, it became clear I didn't know anything concrete enough to begin a search. I didn't want to try to find out where the mother was and bother her. It had been close to 30 years since we had seen or spoken to each other.

Sandy wasn't flustered by this new development at all. She is a very special person. On our very first date in 1966 I told her about this baby. She has always encouraged me to find the child. For years after we were married, Sandy always felt that someday she would be home and get a knock on the door. Upon opening it there would be a full-grown adult asking, "Does Mike MacIntosh live here?"

We prayed about it and let it rest at that. We never expected to hear anything from Karen because it seemed like such an impossibility.

Three months later Sandy was speaking at a pastors' wives conference. Karen happened to be in Sandy's room, going over their notes together. Then Karen said, "Oh, my gosh! I forgot to tell you. I found Mike's baby. It's a girl." Before she had time to react, Sandy looked at her watch and saw that it was time to speak. Of course, she was more than distracted as she tried to communicate with 600 women.

After Sandy finished speaking, she rushed to the nearest pay phone to let me know the baby had been located. "Blown away" would best describe my reaction. The details were sketchy. A birth certificate inscribed with the words "baby girl MacIntosh" had been found. August 19, 1961, was the birthdate.

It was then the love of God showed through most brightly. The occupation of the adoptive father was listed as "theological professor." I was awestruck. Could it be that this child was adopted by a Christian family? So many questions ran through my mind. Would I ever find her? Would she want to know me? Would this be a burden on Sandy? And what about the man and woman who raised the baby? Would I pose a threat or cause pain to them? What about our own five beautiful children? Would this hurt them? Would they be angry or upset if we were to find my long-lost daughter?

Sandy and I chose to move slowly at this point, waiting several weeks to proceed any further. Then we got the family together, went to dinner, told them the news, and received their input. There were all sorts of questions. We closely watched and listened to the differing reactions—but none of our five was offended. They unanimously agreed that I should "go for it" and find their missing sister.

We are a close family, and our kids are all young adults; if one of them had shown or voiced any reluctance in the matter, I would have stopped right there and waited years, if necessary, to proceed. We love and respect all of our children, and Sandy felt that in this matter we must respect their feelings above all.

Next, I methodically began a search of all the theological seminaries in the San Francisco Bay area—again, a monumental task to find a school that might not even exist anymore. And how many institutions would still have employment records going back to the summer of '61? I' knew this was going to take phenomenal effort. Where in the world would I find my daughter? She could live in any of 50 states or a foreign country . . . or she could have died.

That's where good old Tom Gazi came to the rescue. When I told him one night what I was up to, he mentioned that he had a friend who was an expert in finding missing persons. He would be more than happy to call him and see if anything might pop up. In the meantime, I had to go away to school for two weeks to finish up my doctor of ministry degree. Approximately 35 other pastors from various denominations and American cities made up the student body. One day we took turns telling something about ourselves and giving a prayer request. I explained how I was searching for my child, and would they please pray for me and remember me in their prayers? It always helps to have a few dozen good praying ministers on your side!

Christmas came and went, New Year's passed, then Tom called to say he found three families in northern California who fit the profile we were looking for. Did I want to call them? After two numbers were dead ends, Sandy and I sat down in my den, held hands, and prayed. I dialed the number but hung up before anyone answered. I was scared.

I called Karen the next afternoon to ask if she would call and see if this was the couple. She made the call to the home of Dr. Bernard and Juanita Northrup in Redding, California.

"Hello, is Joy Northrup there?"

"Why, no, she's at her house."

"Do you have her number handy?"

"What is this about?"

"It's about a reunion."

"High school?"

"Something like that."

"Here you go."

"Thank you."

Immediately afterward Karen called us. Not only had she found the couple, but she had the telephone number for this 30-year-old "baby girl MacIntosh." Amazing!

There are millions of telephone numbers in the United States, and I possessed one that represented potential disaster or an immediate miracle. I asked Karen if she would make the call for me; I was too nervous. What if my daughter didn't want to see me? What if she carried bitterness all these years that she had been adopted? We knew that Karen would handle the matter wisely.

Less than five minutes later our phone rang. It was Karen. She had spoken to this mystery woman in my life—and discovered she wanted to talk with me. Would I please call her?

Karen gave me her telephone number, and we were astounded to discover she was in our area code, a mere two-hour drive from our house. Unbelievable! When I called, Sandy and I prayed together and sat holding hands.

"Hello, is this Joy?"

"Yes, it is."

"I'm not sure if you're going to like this or not, but this is Mike MacIntosh. I'm your father."

To make a long story short, she liked it!

One of the first things she asked was, "Are you a Christian?"

"Yes, I am."

"You mean, I don't have to evangelize you?"

Not only amazing, but incredible. God not only stopped the bleeding and dressed the hurt, He now was healing it. Trust me, please. If you don't think you can clear up the past, you are absolutely, 100 percent correct! You can't—but God can. God is the Healer, so let Him heal.

The next day I jumped into my car, armed with teddy bears and roses, and drove to meet her. About two miles from her house I was listening to an "oldies but goodies" station. Ironically, a song from my teen years was playing: "Daddy's Home." As I pulled up in front of Joy's home, the song finished with the words "Daddy's home to stay."

For the next several hours we brought each other up to speed on our lives. I wanted to reassure her that she was better off not having been raised by me, a 17-year-old who didn't grow up until he was 26. The terrible sixties combined with a lifestyle that was not conducive to raising children.

She still asserts today that I did most of the talking. She's right—I was afraid I'd never see her again, so I didn't want to leave any historical stones unturned.

Around 2 A.M. we decided it was time to call it a day. Before I left, her husband asked, "Do you have any doubts that Joy is your daughter?" My reply was simple and straightforward: "Well, she looks a lot like her mother, as best as I can remember."

Then he said, "What about the dates? Don't you think the dates have something to do with it?"

The dates he was talking about were as follows:

- My brother David was killed in an automobile accident on August 19; Joy was born on August 19.

- My mother was born on August 12; Joy's old-est daughter was born on August 12.

- I was born on March 26; the previous year Joy had a stillbirth, a full-term baby girl born March 26. Joy named the baby Victoria Michelle; Michelle is French for Michael, my own name.

That's all I needed to hear! She was my daughter, all right.

The great God of creation had watched ever so closely the lives of Michael and Joy and intertwined them in a beautiful mosaic masterpiece. What would the odds be of all those dates matching up together? Oh yes—I guess I should mention that our youngest child, Phillip, was born October 30. One year after meeting Joy, she gave birth to her third daughter, Paige—you guessed it, on October 30. You probably figured out by now that Joy made me an instant grandfather. Tara, Whitney, and Paige—three beautiful young ladies who now have an extra grandfather to love them.

As a side note: Dr. and Mrs. Northrup are quality people. They accepted me into their lives with open arms and loving hearts. We are all friends who marvel at God's handiwork.

One final note: I have the greatest wife in the world. Sandy has accepted Joy and her children as if they were all her own. I think for me that is what makes this all so special. The love that Sandy has for my first daughter truly does reflect the love that God has for all of us.

Yes, God is the Healer. He healed my heart and put it all into perspective for me. His timing was just that: *His* timing. He waited all those years, holding off for just the right time.

And how can I say it was just the right time? When I finally contacted Joy, she and her family had just moved from Florida to California. Her husband had begun a new job, and they didn't know anyone. Her baby had recently died; she herself contracted jaundice. She was tired, depressed, and feeling as if God wasn't there.

At the same time I, too, was tired, worn out from globe-trotting the past 20 years. I had prayed, "God, please show me that You love me. Not because I am a minister. Not just because I am a Christian husband and father. But show me You love me just because of me." I discovered later that Joy had prayed almost the same prayer at just about the same time.

Amazing, isn't it? I hope you have begun to realize that the God of the Bible is the Healer of all your hurts. Did you know that the Bible says, "When my father and my mother forsake me, then the LORD will take me up" (Psalm 27:10 KJV). That scripture sure held true for "baby girl MacIntosh"—a Baptist minister and his wife turned out to embody the loving arms of God. The tenderness of a mother's love was not to come from her own flesh and blood, for the heart of a frightened 18-year-old woman wasn't able to give what Joy needed. Yet God's heart touched Joy through the heart of a godly woman praying for a little girl. The heart of God answered their prayers and filled their lives with a real JOY! It was God's tender touch at work again.

Thank the Lord that He is the Healer. Let God heal even those long-lost hurts and pains you felt as a teenager or adolescent or even as a toddler. He makes all things beautiful in His time.

Time Is Short

Somewhere I came across this anonymous quote that always reminds me time is short. We must enjoy the time we have. It is the most precious commodity given to us. We must allow God to use the time we have to bring us

His love, joy, blessings, inner healing, and encouragement through the painful situations we face. It takes time for Him to bring situations and people together.

If I Had My Life to Live Over

I'd dare to make more mistakes next time,
I'd relax, I would limber up,
I would be sillier than I have been this trip,
I would take fewer things seriously,
I would take more chances,
I would climb more mountains and swim
    more rivers,
I would eat more ice cream and less beans,
I would perhaps have more actual troubles,
But I'd have fewer imaginary ones.

You see, I'm one of those people who live
Sensibly and sanely hour after hour, day after day.
Oh, I've had my moments, and if I had it to do
    over again, I'd have more of them.
In fact, I'd try to do nothing else,
Just moments, one after the other instead of living
    so many years ahead of time.

I've been one of those persons who never go
    anywhere without a thermometer, hot water
    bottle, rain coat and parachute.
If I had to do it again, I would travel lighter than
    I have.
If I had my life to live over,
I would start barefoot earlier in the spring,
And stay that way later in the fall,
I would go to more dinners,
I would ride more merry-go-rounds,
I would pick more daisies.

It's time to smell the flowers and pick more daisies. Call upon God now and ask Him to bring your life into

His perfect timing. Then the right friend, or doctor, or stranger will appear with the right answers, right words, or the right tender touch.

As James 4 says, we must recognize that we don't control our own earthly destinies. Only God knows what the next hour is going to bring our way, so let's learn to let Him follow through with His plan:

> Go to now, ye that say, Today or tomorrow we will go into such a city, and continue there a year, and buy and sell, and get gain: Whereas ye know not what shall be on the morrow. For what is your life? It is even a vapour, that appeareth for a little time, and then vanisheth away. For that ye ought to say, If the Lord will, we shall live, and do this, or that. But now ye rejoice in your boastings: all such rejoicing is evil (James 4:13-16 KJV).

Let us trust the Lord's love to complete the fullness of our healing . . . in *His* time.

15

Two Are Better Than One

—*The Tender Touch of God*—

Friends who care are definitely part of God's healing process.

The way I choose my close friends is pretty simple. I look for people who have been hurt, who know what life is about. I have found that most faithful people have suffered the loss of a loved one or have been through some traumatic situation that left them helpless. This usually humbles a person in a way which makes them value life.

Pain and hurt draw people together. Suffering also humbles a person and makes him or her more understanding of others and their weaknesses. Experiences that hurt should make people softer and, to borrow a famous quote from former president George Bush, "a kinder, gentler people." Men and women who have "hit bottom" in business, marriage, addiction, or whatever, also tend to refrain from hurting other people and, in fact, are powerful agents of healing.

Friends Help Comfort

In writing to the Christians in the city of Corinth, the apostle Paul said:

> Blessed be God, even the Father of our Lord Jesus Christ, the Father of mercies, and the God of all comfort; who comforteth us in all our tribulation, that we may be able to comfort them which are in any trouble, by the comfort wherewith we ourselves are comforted of God (2 Corinthians 1:3,4 KJV).

This text tells us at least four things:

1. God is the Father of mercies.

2. God is the God of all comfort.

3. God comforts in all situations.

4. God enables us through hurt to comfort others as He has comforted us.

Here is a classic description of God's tender touch. He uses a painful situation in my life and comforts me. At the same time He intends that I will now share this comfort with the next person I meet who needs help. Otherwise, I am missing real healing if I do not use what God has brought to my life for the good of others. The question is, Did I learn anything from this? If I did then I will be more than happy to help others and be sensitive to them. And it doesn't even have to be a "big thing" that I do.

Teddy's Story

No other story has touched my heart more than the one I would like to relay to you next. I first came upon it years ago in Chuck Swindoll's book *The Quest for Character.*[1] It illustrates how important a friend can be in the life of someone who is hurting.

Teddy Stallard was disinterested in school. His clothes were wrinkled, and his hair was always messed up. Teddy always wore a deadpan expression, a glassy-eyed countenance, an unfocused stare. He was unattractive, unmotivated, and uncommunicative.

When his teacher, Miss Thompson, spoke to him, Teddy always answered in monosyllables. He was just plain hard to like. Even though his teacher said she loved everyone in her class equally, deep down inside she knew she wasn't being completely truthful.

Whenever she marked Teddy's papers, she got a certain perverse pleasure out of putting X's next to the wrong answers; and when she put the F's at the top of his papers, she always did it with a flair. She should have known better. She had Teddy's records, and she knew more about him than she wanted to admit. The records read:

> First Grade: Teddy shows promise with his work and attitude, but poor home situation.

> Second Grade: Teddy could do better. Mother is seriously ill. He receives little help at home.

> Third Grade: Teddy is a good boy but too serious. He is a slow learner. His mother died this year.

> Fourth Grade: Teddy is very slow, but well-behaved. His father shows no interest.

Christmas came, and the boys and girls in Miss Thompson's class brought her Christmas presents. They piled their presents on her desk and crowded around to watch her open them. Among the presents was a gift from Teddy Stallard. Miss Thompson was surprised that he had brought her a gift, but he had.

Teddy's gift was wrapped in brown paper and was held together with Scotch tape. On the paper were written the simple words, "For Miss Thompson from Teddy." When she opened Teddy's present, out fell a gaudy rhinestone bracelet (with half the stones missing) and a bottle of cheap perfume.

The other boys and girls began to giggle and smirk over Teddy's gifts, but Miss Thompson at least had enough sense to silence them by immediately putting on the bracelet and dabbing some of the perfume on her wrist. Holding her wrist up for the other children to smell, she said, "Doesn't it smell lovely?" And the children, taking their cue from the teacher, readily agreed with "Ooh's" and "Ah's."

At the end of the day, when school was over and the other children had left, Teddy lingered behind. He slowly came over to his teacher's desk and said softly, "Miss Thompson . . . Miss Thompson, you smell just like my mother . . . and her bracelet looks real pretty on you, too. I'm glad you liked my presents."

When Teddy left, Miss Thompson got down on her knees and asked God to forgive her. The next day when the children came to school, they were welcomed by a new teacher. Miss Thompson had become a different person. She was no longer just a teacher; she had become an agent of God.

She was now a person committed to loving her children and doing things for them that would live on after her. She helped all the children, but especially Teddy

Stallard. By the end of that school year, Teddy showed dramatic improvement. He had caught up with most of the students and was even ahead of some.

She didn't hear from Teddy for a long time. Then one day, she received a note that read:

> Dear Miss Thompson:
> I wanted you to be the first to know. I will be graduating second in my class.
>
> Love,
> Teddy Stallard

Four years later, another note came:

> Dear Miss Thompson:
> They just told me I will be graduating first in my class. I wanted you to be the first to know. The university has not been easy, but I liked it.
>
> Love,
> Teddy Stallard

And four years later another note:

> Dear Miss Thompson:
> As of today, I am Theodore Stallard, M.D. How about that? I wanted you to be the first to know. I am getting married next month, the 27th to be exact. I want you to come and sit where my mother would sit if she were alive. You are the only family I have now; Dad died last year.
>
> Love,
> Teddy Stallard

Miss Thompson went to that wedding, and she sat where Teddy's mother would have sat.

That story almost says it all, don't you think? Without friends, the Teddy Stallards of this world get left behind.

Tragically, they also get stepped on or thrown away. I am sure that many members of today's gangs have backgrounds similar to Teddy's. Miss Thompson chose to love Teddy and understand him. This boy's life was healed simply because a friend cared enough to comfort him.

You Mean I Don't Have to Shoot Myself?

A couple of years ago I drove from San Diego to Orange County to have lunch with an old friend I hadn't seen for three or four years. The hour-and-thirty-minute drive gave me time to think and daydream. I remembered things that we had done together in the ministry. I remembered how he financially helped my family when we were in need.

After lunch we went to his office and I told him about the work we were doing with kids. He was interested in the National Youth Crisis Hotline, so I told him he could monitor a call with me. I dialed my access code, and we came into the middle of a counseling session. All we heard for a couple of minutes was sobbing and crying. Then a teenage girl's voice spoke.

"You mean . . . you mean . . . if I put the gun down and don't shoot myself, you will be my friend?"

We had happened upon a suicide call. Apparently, the girl had problems so big she couldn't face them alone and planned to shoot herself. Instead, before she pulled the trigger she called 1-800-HIT-HOME and on the other line was a sympathetic and compassionate ear. One who became a friend.

It was the lack of friends that made this desperate young woman consider suicide. Her loneliness had eaten away at her for a long time. Fortunately, she listened to wise counsel, put the gun down, and went next door to a neighbor's house to ask for help. From there the counselor talked with her in the presence of an adult and was able to defuse the situation without a tragic mishap.

Friends, true friends, listen to us. We can ramble on for hours about nothing significant, and then when we finally get around to spilling our guts, they're still all ears. That speeds along the healing process for all of us.

So talk with a friend. Tell him or her the whole story. Let your friends know how you are really feeling and what led up to this difficult time you are in. Remember, there's nothing like a friend to help bear a burden.

Friendly Words of Wisdom

The Bible has many verses about friends. Let's take a few moments and look at some of these "friendly words of wisdom."

"A friend loves at all times" (Proverbs 17:17).

"Faithful are the wounds of a friend" (Proverbs 27:6).

"Do not forsake your own friend or your father's friend" (Proverbs 27:10).

A friend should show pity (Job 6:14).

"Two are better than one" (Ecclesiastes 4:9-12).

Don't weary your friends (Proverbs 25:17; 27:14).

The poor don't have many friends (Proverbs 14:20).

Gossip can separate even the chiefest of friends (Proverbs 16:28; 17:9).

The sweetness of a friend's hearty counsel rejoices the heart (Proverbs 27:9).

Abraham was the friend of God (2 Chronicles 20:7; Isaiah 41:8).

Jonathan was a friend to David (1 Samuel 20:30-33; 23:16,17; 2 Samuel 1:26).

Hushai stood by David in his trial (2 Samuel 15:31-37; 16:15-23).

Cornelius called his friends together to hear the gospel (Acts 10:24).

The Bible also tells us that Jesus Christ is an awesome role model of a friend. He is the friend who sticks closer than a brother (Proverbs 18:24) and a friend of sinners (Matthew 11:19).

Although Jesus definitely was recognized by His disciples as the leader, teacher, and master, there came a time when Jesus Himself said His relationship to the disciples was about to transition to something else. Read the words of the apostle John as he records the scene:

This is My commandment, that you love one another as I have loved you. Greater love has no one than this, than to lay down one's life for his friends. You are My friends if you do whatever I command you. No longer do I call you servants, for a servant does not know what his master is doing; but I have called you friends, for all things that I heard from My Father I have made known to you (John 15:12-15).

Isn't that wonderful, to know that Jesus sees people as His friends? He does not think of Himself as king with us His serfs, or as a superstar with us His groupies. Our Lord and Savior took pains to call us His friends. And what a tremendous Friend He is!

We All Need Friends

Friends are the greatest, and you need them. Without friends we become lonely. A study by the American Council of Life Insurance reported that the most lonely group in America is college students. That's almost hard to believe. With all of the parties, school teams to follow, and so many people in their classes to meet—that's surprising! Next on the list are divorced people, welfare recipients, single mothers, rural students, housewives, and the elderly.

It is easy to see that without friends, life can be more difficult than it needs to be. When the business goes bad, you need a friend to talk with. After the divorce, you need a friend to help you with the pain. When death has visited your family, friends make the difference.

Today I spoke on the phone with a man in our church whose wife died yesterday. The funeral services are tomorrow. "How are you making it?" I asked. He responded with confidence and assurance, "The people from my home fellowship are being just great." Our church has about 125 home fellowships. Bible study, worship, prayer, and the bonding of friends happen so much better in a small, close-knit group. It is these friends from the church who are helping to carry the weight of this man's tragedy. They are living out the command of Galatians 6:2, which says, "Bear one another's burdens, and so fulfill the law of Christ."

Someone anonymously penned these words: "Friendship doubles our joy and divides our grief." Isn't it a great feeling when you are sick and a friend calls or comes by to check up and see if he can help? Or when the garage needs cleaning and the bedroom a fresh coat of paint, how wonderful it is that friends drop in and help us. The task seems so simple with their input. It seems that time flies when two or three people talk and laugh while doing an undesirable chore.

Recently, some friends in Colorado gave us the use of their house. We could never afford to rent such a beautiful house, but they offered it to us free of charge. What a thrill to have most of our children and granddaughters together under the same roof, with a 360-degree view of the Rocky Mountains and snow everywhere. What a joy to ski with my grown kids and to read stories and color with my precious granddaughters. One whole week of laughter, love, and family. No problems to solve, no disgruntled people to appease, no emergencies, no budgets, no pressure. Just love, joy, and peace. We laughed late into the night. Giggled early in the morning. Relaxed in the spa. Played in the snow. Prayed at the same dinner table. It was a slice of heaven.

The week after our return I saw the owner of the home at a board meeting. Marsh is such a loving, generous, and gracious man (the same characteristics go for his wife, Debbie). I told him that our kids were all writing a personal letter to thank him and his wife for the tremendous time our family had together in their home. He humbly bowed his head and said contritely, "I wish they wouldn't do that." He and his wife have dedicated their Rocky Mountain paradise to God and His servants. He didn't want any recognition; he just wanted to bless us as a friend.

Marsh understands that it is "more blessed to give than to receive." Friends enjoy blessing one another, and we have to learn how to receive their grace gracefully.

Yellow Roses for a Friend

Henry Penn, former president of the Society of American Florists, tells what he calls one of the most memorable incidents of his life as a florist.[2] One day two boys and a girl about ten years of age made a visit to his store. They wore ragged clothes but had clean faces and hands. The boys took off their caps when they entered the shop. One of them stepped forward and said solemnly, "We're the committee, and we'd like some very nice yellow flowers."

Penn showed them some inexpensive spring flowers, but the boy said, "I think we'd like something better than that."

"Do they have to be yellow?" asked Penn.

"Yes, sir," came the reply.

"Mickey would like them even better if they were yellow because he had a yellow sweater."

"Are these for a funeral?" the florist asked quietly.

The boy nodded while the girl turned to keep back the tears.

"She's his sister," the boy explained. "He was a good kid. A truck . . . yesterday . . . he was playing in the street. We saw it happen."

Then the other boy added, "Us kids took up a collection. We got 18 cents. Would roses cost an awful lot, mister? Yellow roses?"

Touched by the story of the tragedy and the loyalty and love and friendship of these youngsters, Penn replied, "I have some nice yellow roses here that I'm selling for 18 cents a dozen."

"Gee, those would be swell!" exclaimed one of the boys.

"Mickey would like those," the other one confirmed.

"I'll make up a nice spray," promised the sympathetic florist, "with ferns and a ribbon. Where shall I send them?"

"Would it be all right, mister, if we took 'em now?" asked one of the boys.

"We'd kinda like to take 'em over and give 'em to Mickey ourselves. He'd like it better that way."

Penn accepted the 18 cents, and the "committee," carrying the kind of flowers "Mickey would like," walked out of the shop. Said Penn, "I felt uplifted for days. Unbeknownst to them, I had a part in their tribute to their friend." And friends had helped a sister come to grips with her deep grief.

Let the Bud Bloom

It is so important in receiving the tender touch of God to allow the love of friends to enter your situation. Let them love you by serving you and helping you through the difficulties you face. Let them use their gifts to serve you. Maybe you have just gotten out of the hospital. You may feel awkward with attention, but your friends want to show their love by cooking dinner for your family or by doing the laundry. Let them do it. Remember, Jesus had help carrying His cross up the hill to Golgotha. Be willing to receive the help of a friend. Ringo Starr made a lot of money singing "I get by with a little help from my friends." He not only got wealthy, but on this point he was right.

Friendship is a great healing tool the Lord uses in our lives. Let friendship bud forth into beautiful bloom. Accept the help of the ones who love you the most, and let them freely love you back to health. You know that you would do the same for them.

My friend John Dahlberg came into my life when my health fell to an all-time low a few years ago. His generosity and concern were major factors in expediting my healing. God has blessed him with a very successful business and a beautiful wife and children.

John loves the ocean. He lives on the bay and has a boat moored at a dock in back of his house. One day while we were on vacation he offered to have his captain take my family for a cruise (he and his family were out of town). My first reaction was that I couldn't even afford the fuel to get from his dock to the jetty, yet he and his wife, Marilyn, wanted to share their blessings with Sandy and me. Finally, we took him up on the offer and our family jumped on board and cruised south from Newport Beach to Dana Point, California, for lunch. After a super brunch at a dockside restaurant, we headed out to sea. The day seemed made in heaven—sunny, 80 degrees, and calm seas.

Captain Brent said, "I think we will go offshore about a mile to see if we can find some dolphins." Find some dolphins! Did we ever find some dolphins. All of a sudden, pods of dolphins shot out of the water from every direction—hundreds of dolphins. Ten to 20 were riding the huge wake on both sides aft of the boat. At all times we saw five dolphins side by side and switching turns at the bow with three or four dozen on both sides racing with us at full speed.

It was so beautiful and exciting. We rode for close to an hour, enjoying our newfound friends. All of our children joined me in shouting and screaming at the top of our lungs. We had the time of our lives. It was a one-in-a-million experience.

While standing alone at the bow, I looked back and saw how happy Sandy and the children were. I bowed my head and thanked Jesus for sending this school—no, this university of dolphins—to bring us such joy. Then I thanked Him for our dear friends John and Marilyn. They knew how tired I was, and they wanted to bless us. They sure did!

If you are tired, burned out, or in great pain, remember that the joy of friendship can bring tremendous healing power into your life. Good friends can expedite your recovery. Above all, remember that Jesus is your best friend, and it blesses Him to see you and your friends love one another. His tender touch often comes to us through friends. So be a friend, and allow your friends to bless you through their love.

Have you seen the Ten Commandments of Friendship? I don't know who wrote them, but they're so good I thought I'd reproduce them here:

ONE: Speak to people—there is nothing as nice as a cheerful word of greeting.

TWO: Smile at people—it takes 72 muscles to frown, but only 14 to smile!

THREE: Call people by name—the sweetest music to anyone's ear is the sound of their own name.

FOUR: Be friendly and helpful—if you would have friends, be friendly.

FIVE: Be cordial—speak and act as if everything you do were a real pleasure.

SIX: Be genuinely interested in people—you can like everyone IF YOU TRY.

SEVEN: Be generous with praise; cautious with criticism.

EIGHT: Be considerate of the feelings of others—it will be appreciated.

NINE: Be thoughtful of the opinions of others.

TEN: Be alert to give service—what counts most in life is what we do for others!

16

Glimpses of Heaven

The Tender Touch of God

One of the worst hurts we can carry around with us is the loss of a loved one. Death is a tremendous mystery, as is "after death"—a subject which several authors over the past 20 years have tried to tackle. The near-death experience has been the topic both of controversy and much research.

People who claim to have undergone near-death experiences very often tell of a mysterious white light at the end of a tunnel. Some of these stories leave us confused or full of doubt. We wonder, *Is that what heaven is really like?*

These accounts contrast with the sterile images many people have of heaven, full of people dressed in white robes floating through the sky on white, puffy clouds.

When some of us try to picture heaven, we think of halos overhead and golden harps in each person's hands—not too exciting for the adventurous type.

We can't help wondering, *Is any of that what heaven is really like? Can we know anything about heaven before we get there?* A lot of people—even Christians—doubt that we can.

D.L. Moody on Heaven

Thousands of souls throughout England and the United States are in heaven today because of the life and message of D.L. Moody. His ministry at the end of the nineteenth century profoundly impacted the English-speaking world.

It is probable that Moody preached on the subject of heaven more frequently than on any other subject in his long evangelistic ministry. One evening he was on his way to preach when a friend asked him, "Mr. Moody, what are you going to preach about?"

"I am going to preach about heaven," he replied. When a scowl crossed the face of his friend, Moody asked, "What makes you look so?"

"Why, your subject of heaven. What's the use of talking upon a subject that's all speculation? It's only wasting time on a subject about which you can only speculate."

Moody answered, "If the Lord doesn't want us to speak about heaven, He would never have told us about such a place in the Scriptures; and, as Timothy says, 'All the Scriptures are given by inspiration, and all parts are profitable.'"

That evening in a message titled "Heaven and Who Are There," Moody said:

There's no part of the Word of God that is not profitable, and I believe if men would read more carefully these Scriptures, they would think more of heaven. If we want to get men to fix their hearts and attention upon heaven, we must get them to read more about it. Men who say that heaven is a speculation have not read their Bibles. In the blessed Bible there are allusions scattered all through it. If I were to read to you all the passages upon heaven from Genesis to Revelation, it would take me all night and tomorrow to do it. When I took some of the passages lately and showed them to a lady, "Why," said she, "I didn't think there was so much about heaven in the Bible."

If I were to go into a foreign land and spend my days there, I would like to know all about it; its climate, its inhabitants, their customs, their privileges, their government. I would find nothing about that land that would not interest me. Suppose you all were going away to Africa, to Germany, to China, and were going to make one of those places your home, and suppose that I had just come from one of those countries; how eagerly you would listen to what I had to say. I can imagine how the old, gray-haired men and the young men and the deaf would crowd around and put up their hands to learn something about it.

But there is a country in which you are going to spend your whole future, and you are listless about what kind of a country it is. My friends, where are you going to spend eternity?[1]

I wonder, have you ever pondered the nature of where you are going to spend eternity? This is not idle speculation; in fact, the Bible tells us a great deal about heaven. For one thing, Scripture makes it clear that in heaven we shall experience the complete healing of all our aches and pains. But it goes much further than that.

It gives us several glimpses into what heaven is really like.

Let's take a moment to look at heaven. It is one of those subjects which most people don't really understand. Yet when we gain a clear grasp of the truth concerning heaven, we will find it easier to relax.

What Does the Bible Say?

Charles H. Spurgeon, the great British expositor of the nineteenth century, once said to his students, "When you talk about heaven, let your face light up with a heavenly glory. When you tell about hell, your everyday face will do."

The faces of the apostles Paul and John certainly lit up when they talked about heaven. Their insights can help us understand more about our future home.

In 2 Corinthians 12, Paul tells us that he knew a man (we can presume it was Paul himself), in the body or out of the body he didn't know, who was taken up into the third heaven and saw things that were unutterable. What is this "third heaven"?

The first heaven is our sky and our atmosphere, where the birds fly. By using aircraft, man is capable of flying in the first heaven.

The second heaven is the universe beyond us. It is where our solar system orbits our sun in the midst of a galaxy known as the Milky Way—only one of innumerable galaxies moving through space. Scientists tell us that our universe, which makes up all of the second heaven, is approximately 15 billion light-years across. A light-year is the distance light travels in a year. The speed of light is 186,000 miles per second. Multiply that by 60 seconds; then multiply that by 60 minutes; then multiply that by 24 hours in a day. Now you know how far light travels in one day. Finally, multiply that number by 365, and you will have the number of miles in a single light-year. Now multiply that number by 15 billion—and you get the picture that we are but a speck in a vast universe.

Somewhere beyond the boundaries of our known universe is the third heaven, in which the Lord sits and reigns upon His throne. More than likely, this is what Paul meant when he said he was taken up into the third heaven. Naturally, the things he saw there were "unutterable." How could he describe what he saw? The beauty and the glory of heaven was so breathtaking that Paul simply could find no words to express its magnificence. No matter what language he might have chosen, there was no earthly word that could begin to describe heaven's most insignificant detail.

In this passage, Paul reminds us that heaven is not some figment of our imagination. Quite the contrary, it is a very real place. It is not some "pie in the sky in the great by-and-by," but rather is a beautiful, eternal place prepared for God's children.

In the book of Revelation, the apostle John described his own amazing vision of the eternal city called the New Jerusalem. He tells us that not only was God willing to let His Son die for our sins to give us eternal life, but He also has designed a sinless city for us beyond all imagination. Read the apostle's description in Revelation 21:10-26(KJV):

> And he carried me away in the spirit to a great and high mountain, and shewed me that great city, the holy Jerusalem, descending out of heaven from God, having the glory of God: and her light was like unto a stone most precious, even like a jasper stone, clear as crystal; and had a wall great and high, and had twelve gates, and at the gates twelve angels, and names written thereon, which are the names of the twelve tribes of the children of Israel: on the east three gates; on the north three gates; on the south three gates; and on the west three gates. And the

wall of the city had twelve foundations, and in them the names of the twelve apostles of the Lamb.

And he that talked with me had a golden reed to measure the city, and the gates thereof, and the wall thereof. And the city lieth foursquare, and the length is as large as the breadth: and he measured the city with the reed, twelve thousand furlongs. The length and the breadth and the height of it are equal. And he measured the wall thereof, an hundred and forty and four cubits, according to the measure of a man, that is, of the angel.

And the building of the wall of it was of jasper: and the city was pure gold, like unto clear glass. And the foundations of the wall of the city were garnished with all manner of precious stones. The first foundation was jasper; the second, sapphire; the third, a chalcedony; the fourth, an emerald; the fifth, sardonyx; the sixth, sardius; the seventh, chrysolite; the eighth, beryl; the ninth, a topaz; the tenth, a chrysoprasus; the eleventh, a jacinth; the twelfth, an amethyst. And the twelve gates were twelve pearls; every several gate was of one pearl: and the street of the city was pure gold, as it were transparent glass.

And I saw no temple therein: for the Lord God Almighty and the Lamb are the temple of it. And the city had no need of the sun, neither of the moon, to shine in it: for the glory of God did lighten it, and the Lamb is the light thereof. And the nations of them which are saved shall walk in the light of it: and the kings of the earth do bring their glory and honour into it. And the gates of it shall not be shut at all by day: for there shall be no night there. And they shall bring the glory and honour of the nations into it.

Try to imagine the beauty and the splendor of your future home. Not only is it breathtaking, it is also beautifully awesome.

This city is shaped like a cube, 1500 miles long, 1500 miles wide, and 1500 miles high. Heaven is huge, and it has plenty of room for both you and your loved ones.

The gates are made of pearl with an angel guarding each one. The foundation of the wall is constructed in 12 layers, each layer a beautiful stone or gem. The city's streets are paved with pure gold, transparent as glass, while crystal-clear water runs from the throne of God through the middle of the street. That's got to be heaven! (There aren't many clean rivers left today.)

John described the attributes of heaven precisely, probably to give us hope for the future. Listen to more of his description of what lies ahead for us:

> And I saw a new heaven and a new earth: for the first heaven and the first earth were passed away; and there was no more sea. And I John saw the holy city, new Jerusalem, coming down from God out of heaven, prepared as a bride adorned for her husband. And I heard a great voice out of heaven saying, Behold, the tabernacle of God is with men, and he will dwell with them, and they shall be his people, and God himself shall be with them, and be their God. And God shall wipe away all tears from their eyes; and there shall be no more death, neither sorrow, nor crying, neither shall there be any more pain: for the former things are passed away. And he that sat upon the throne said, Behold, I make all things new. And he said unto me, Write: for these words are true and faithful (Revelation 21:1-5).

Isn't that amazing? To think that God personally will wipe away all tears from our eyes! You know as well as I do that we don't let too many people touch our faces, let alone wipe tears away. Yet that is precisely what God will do for each of His children.

God is a very personal God, and He will spend time alone with all of us. Tears of joy and thanksgiving will flow out of our eyes when we enter heaven. To see His glory and His love will be overwhelming. God is very concerned about us. He is a very sensitive and personal God.

Some people worry that they might not recognize loved ones when they get to heaven. But there's little reason for such concern. One day G. Campbell Morgan, an outstanding expositor of the last generation and the pastor of a thriving church in England, was asked, "Do you think we will know our loved ones in heaven?" Dr. Morgan, in his truly British manner, answered, "I do not expect to be a bigger fool in heaven than I am here, and I know my loved ones here."

One of the best things about heaven is that all death, sorrow, and crying will be done away with for God's children. And above all, we see those great words, "neither shall there be any more pain." Heaven is painless. God lives in a painless environment, and He wants you to come home with Him. In heaven, pain will be gone forever. Now, that's great news, isn't it?

Recently while speaking at one of our crusade outreaches, I met a couple whose son had committed suicide the previous year. After the message, the man and woman asked me, "Did you know that we lost our son last year?" I acknowledged that I did. Then I asked them if I could pray for them. The three of us stood with our arms around each other, thanking God that heaven is not far away and that God's love for this mother and father was real and present. The tears that flowed were sweet tears from a husband and wife who needed to be reassured of each other's love and also of the love of God.

How wonderful it was to see this man bring his daughter to the meeting the next night. When she, too, heard the good news, her heart couldn't contain the hurt another minute. Not only had her brother died the previous year, but she and her husband had divorced. Apparently the pain of the back-to-back incidents caused her to with-draw into herself and break off communication with others.

Two days after receiving Jesus into her life, she and her dad were at the bookstore getting books about Jesus and buying Christian music tapes. Thank God there really is a world without pain waiting for us. What a relief to never again worry about being hurt!

In John 14, Jesus told us that He was going to heaven to prepare a place for us. He described our "place" as a mansion. It has always amazed me that it is a mansion, not just a home or house. It's definitely not a pup tent, condo, apartment, or Winnebago. A mansion is what He said, and that's what I am going to expect.

Not too long ago one of our daughters and her husband were buying a house. Sandy and I were able to give them some money for a down payment. The incident reminded me that for our new home in heaven we won't need any down payment, escrow, or filing fees. There will be no closing costs, insurance, utilities, repairs, or worry about being served with foreclosure or eviction papers. Jesus has gone to prepare a place for us, and the total price already has been paid.

How Do We Get to Heaven?

It's wonderful to know a little about heaven, but how is it that we get there in the first place? Do we work extra hard at being nice? Do we need to give the church money? Just what qualifies people to be allowed into heaven?

A little boy, caught in mischief by his mother, was asked: "How do you expect to get into heaven?" He thought a moment and then said, "Well, I'll just run in and out and in and out and keep slamming the door until they say, 'For goodness sake, come in or stay out.' Then I'll go in."

Heaven is a very misunderstood place. Some people, like that little boy, think they can go in and out of heaven at will. But according to the Bible, there is only one way to get to heaven.

1. *We first must recognize that there is a path that leads us to heaven.*

Jesus Christ said, "Enter by the narrow gate; for wide is the gate and broad is the way that leads to destruction, and there are many who go in by it. Because narrow is the gate and difficult is the way which leads to life, and there are few who find it" (Matthew 7:13,14).

Jesus told us that more people choose the broad road that leads to destruction than the narrow road that leads to heaven. How sad to think that this broad and easy way is so cleverly disguised that people actually believe it is the road to life. In reality the road leads only to eternal destruction. Oh, how clever the devil is. We must ask ourselves, "Am I on the right path?"

2. *We must realize that there is a registry for the population of heaven.*

In writing to the Philippian church, the apostle Paul said, "And I urge you also, true companion, help these women who labored with me in the gospel, with Clement also, and the rest of my fellow workers, whose names are in the Book of Life" (Philippians 4:3).

It is this Book of Life that we are interested in. Jesus also spoke of this book. In the letters to the seven churches of Asia, Jesus said:

> He who overcomes shall be clothed in white garments, and I will not blot out his name from the Book of Life; but I will confess his name before My Father and before His angels (Revelation 3:5).

Later in the book of Revelation we read of the judgment time and its relationship to this Book of Life:

> And I saw the dead, small and great, standing before God, and books were opened. And another book was opened, which is the Book of Life. And the dead were judged according to their works, by the things which were written in the books (Revelation 20:12).

Please notice that the works of those judged are found in the "books" (plural). This leads us to believe that there are volumes of material for each of our lives. Could these books record our every thought, action, or deed? Could they contain the account of our lives, from birth to death? Whatever is recorded in these books, it is enough to damn us to hell:

> The sea gave up the dead who were in it, and Death and Hades delivered up the dead who were in them. And they were judged, each one according to his works. Then Death and Hades were cast into the lake of fire. This is the second death. And anyone not found written in the Book of Life was cast into the lake of fire (Revelation 20:13-15).

It is imperative that we have our names written in this Book of Life if we wish to enter heaven. Read the following verse and see how strongly this is emphasized:

> But there shall by no means enter it anything that defiles, or causes an abomination or a lie, but only those who are written in the Lamb's Book of Life (Revelation 21:27).

The Lamb is none other than Jesus Himself. If we belong to Him, then our names shall be found in this most important of all books. This is why we need to receive Jesus Christ into our lives by faith.

Years ago I received a letter from an organization telling me that I was coming up in the world and was about to be publicly recognized as a successful man. I had been chosen to be in *Who's Who in the West*. Some time afterward I was invited to be in *Who's Who in America*. Now, two years later, I have received an invitation to be in *Who's Who in the World*. Of course, I realize by now that the gimmick is to flatter you into thinking you are famous so you will buy several of the books as gifts for family and friends. For a few more hundred dollars you can get plaques to hang on your wall to impress the uninformed. The first time around I bought the ego booster, but that was it. (I wonder if I can be in *Who's Who in the Milky Way Galaxy*?)

You don't need to have your name written in any of these *Who's Who* books to make it into heaven. But the Lamb's Book of Life is something else entirely. You might say it's the *Who's Who of Heaven*. And you most assuredly want your name written there.

3. *We must find the right path to heaven.*

What is the right path to heaven? This must be one of the most-often-asked questions of a minister. People always wonder how they can get to heaven.

If you have ever taken a tour to Israel, you know that Israeli tour-bus drivers drive fast and take chances that would never occur to a normal human. Our guide last year tried to calm the nerves of our group after a close brush with an approaching bus. He told us a story:

> A pastor and an Israeli tour-bus driver went to heaven. The driver got a beautiful mansion with large rooms. The pastor got only a one-room bungalow. So he went to St. Peter and asked, "How

come I got such a small house and the bus driver got such a mansion? I've preached the gospel all of my life!" St. Peter replied, "When you preached, the people fell asleep; but when the bus driver drove his tour groups around, every one of them was praying furiously."

The Bible insists there is only one way to heaven, and that way is through Jesus. Jesus Himself gave us these words of instruction in John 14:3-6:

> "And if I go and prepare a place for you, I will come again and receive you to Myself; that where I am, there you may be also. And where I go you know, and the way you know." Thomas said to Him, "Lord, we do not know where You are going, and how can we know the way?" Jesus said to him, "I am the way, the truth, and the life. No one comes to the Father except through Me."

For many years before my conversion I read the Eastern mystics and the writings of Zen, Buddha, and his Western rewrites. They tried to convince me that God is like the hub of a wheel and religion is the spokes leading to the hub, and life is the wheel. I'll tell you what. If you want to believe that shallow nonsense, you'll find that your wheel has a flat tire. How easy and undisciplined we have to be to pick any spoke we want!

No, there is only one way to God, and that is Jesus. He will lead you safely to heaven. In fact, He's the only One who can. Heaven is calling, so receive the blessed invitation and plan now for the trip.

No Worries but Immortality

There is a place for us beyond earth. To know of this future abode will speed the healing process for us. It also will give us hope to know that such a beautiful place is

245

set aside for us, where all pain, sorrow, and suffering has been done away with forever.

At age 39, former heavyweight boxing champion Mohammed Ali announced he was going to make another comeback. He was asked if he was doing so just to stay in the spotlight. "Ain't worried about money. . . . Ain't worried about nothin' but being immortal!"

Immortality is the only thing Mohammed Ali was worried about. How about you? If you are a Christian, God has it all planned out for you. Nothing for you to worry about; it is all taken care of. You shall have immortality in a new body in a painless, eternal city.

A few hours before Dwight L. Moody died, he caught a glimpse of the glory awaiting him. Awakening from a sleep, he said, "Earth recedes, heaven opens before me. If this is death, it is sweet! There is no valley here. God is calling me, and I must go!" His son standing by his bedside said, "No, no, father, you are dreaming."

"No," said Mr. Moody, "I am not dreaming; I have been within the gates; I have seen the children's faces." A short time elapsed and then, following what seemed to the family to be the death struggle, he spoke again: "This is my triumph; this my coronation day! It is glorious!"[2]

Yes, it was glorious. And it can be just as glorious for you.

17

God the Healer

The Tender Touch of God

F ew people in history have suffered more than Job. His story is told in one of the oldest books in the Bible. If the tale were retold today by James Michener or some other modern author, it would probably become an all-time bestseller. If it were a motion picture, it would sweep the Oscars.

I have yet to meet anyone whose troubles come in a close second to Job. If you ever wish to feel good about your problems, then open the Old Testament and read his story. You will shout for joy because your problems will seem so small in comparison.

Job was a godly man who withstood every evil tragedy that the devil could throw at him. Satan stole all his livestock, took away his real estate, killed all his children, massacred all his servants, and finally afflicted Job with boils from the top of his head to the soles of his feet. In the midst of his troubles his wife told him to give up and curse God, while his best friends told him God was judging him because of sin in his life. Job was the wealthiest man in the known world at the time, but he lost it all. He was the most influential man in the known world, but he lost it all. Yet never once did he turn away from God. He is a magnificent study of personal depth and character. Before he knew how his story would turn out, he declared, "Though He slay me, yet will I trust Him" (Job 13:15). And in the depths of his misery, Job said to God, "I know that You can do everything, and that no purpose of Yours can be withheld from You" (Job 42:2).

Healing Belongs to God

In this book we have discussed the role we play in stopping our bleeding and dressing the wounds in our lives, but we must always remember that God is the Healer. Only He can bring full recovery. Job saw this so clearly. He knew God could do anything He wanted to do, that the Lord could just say the word and Job's problems would end immediately. He also recognized that God was invincible. Therefore, he would trust the unseen God he loved instead of surrendering to the situations and conditions in which he found himself.

The book of Job reminds us that life isn't really about us at all; it is about God. Job knew that God was faithful and true, and it was from this basis that he held on for dear life. We must do what he did when God allows our own lives to be tested. Yet it's not easy for us.

I came across a cute story the other day that touched my heart. It spoke so clearly concerning our fears and reminded me of the words of Jesus, "You must become like little children." So often we misread difficult situations and make hasty judgments or decisions. We need to be more like little children who simply trust God.

At the height of the segregation storm, a first-grader was assigned to a newly integrated school. By the end of the day her anxious mother met her at the door to inquire, "How did everything go, honey?"

"Oh, Mother! You know what? A little black girl sat next to me!"

In fear and trepidation, the mother asked, "And what happened?"

"We were both so scared that we held hands all day."

We adults are often like those little girls. It seems as if we are in a big, cruel world that just doesn't care. So what can we do? Grab the Lord's big hand and hold on every day. He will heal these hurts of yours. That's what He's best at—healing and binding up the brokenhearted. Yet the Bible tells us that Jesus once got into a lot of trouble for saying just that.

Trouble in Capernaum

Centuries before Jesus was born, the prophet Isaiah had written:

> The Spirit of the Lord God is upon me; because the Lord hath anointed me to preach good tidings unto the meek; he hath sent me to bind up the brokenhearted, to proclaim liberty to the captives, and the opening of the prison to them that are bound (Isaiah 61:1 KJV).

According to the Gospel of Luke:

> Jesus returned in the power of the Spirit into Galilee: and there went out a fame of him through all the region round about. And he taught in their synagogues, being glorified of all. And he came to Nazareth, where he had been brought up: and, as

his custom was, he went into the synagogue on the sabbath day, and stood up for to read.

And there was delivered unto him the book of the prophet Esaias. And when he had opened the book, he found the place where it was written, The Spirit of the Lord is upon me, because he hath anointed me to preach the gospel to the poor; he hath sent me to heal the brokenhearted, to preach deliverance to the captives, and recovering of sight to the blind, to set at liberty them that are bruised, to preach the acceptable year of the Lord.

And he closed the book, and he gave it again to the minister, and sat down. And the eyes of all them that were in the synagogue were fastened on him. And he began to say unto them, This day is this scripture fulfilled in your ears. And all bare him witness, and wondered at the gracious words which proceeded out of his mouth. And they said, Is not this Joseph's son? (Luke 4:14-22 KJV).

They did not want to hear what Jesus had to say. In the middle of His address they took Him outside the city and tried to push Him over a cliff because they said He was a false prophet. The people couldn't bring themselves to believe that Jesus could be the One whom Isaiah spoke about. Jesus, the One who would heal brokenhearted people? The One who would deliver the captives from their addictive appetites? The One who would break the chains that bound them to sin and to the hurts of this world?

Yes, that's exactly who Jesus is. Jesus Himself said, "They that are whole have no need of the physician, but they that are sick: I came not to call the righteous, but sinners to repentance." He is the Healer, and we must let Him heal our broken lives. It is imperative that we do so.

Let us never forget that God is the Healer. He can as easily mend broken bones as He can broken hearts. It is all within His power. Trust God. He will work a miracle for you . . . if you will only let Him.

Different Healings, Same God

There are countless types of wounds and hurts, and just as many ways of dressing them. In each type of wound, the healing process is different. Though your hurt is very painful, it is more than likely that other people have experienced the same kind of hurt. Yet in your case, the method God uses to begin the healing process may be different from what He used with others.

It may surprise self-starters, type A personalities, and motivated, success-oriented people, but God is at the center of their healing, not themselves. Strong-minded and strong-willed people may think they have to "bite the bullet," "see the job through," to push themselves through this hurt, but attitudes that say, "It will go away," "I'm okay, you're okay" don't always get the job done. It's a lie that God helps those who help themselves. That's not a scriptural position. If anything, the Bible tells us that God helps those who admit they *can't* help themselves.

I find it interesting that a close variation of this self-help philosophy was around in the first century. After Jesus had read the verse from Isaiah to those in the synagogue, He knew what they were thinking and He said, "Ye will surely say unto me this proverb, Physician, heal thyself." That is, do it Yourself, Jesus; heal Yourself.

Thank God we don't have to heal ourselves. God is the Healer. So let's allow Him to do His healing work. He knows what He's doing.

Healing at Last

When I started writing this book almost two years ago, I had an abnormal amount of pain in my back. Since that time I have undergone several medical examinations to "stop the bleeding," so to speak. Tests showed I had mild arthritis in my upper spine, while two of my lower discs were in the early stages of disintegrating. These discs push against my spinal cord and pinch nerves. Finally, some new X rays from a different angle showed that my last vertebra is compressed and twisted.

This knowledge has increased my ability to understand why I have been hurting all day and night. Armed with this new information, I have been able to "stop the bleeding" and have moved on to the next step, to dress the wound.

Now that I know the source of my pain, it is easier to treat the problem. Scott Legitt, director of Ortho Med, the physical rehab center for the University of California, spent hours with me on new computerized machines to help me strengthen my back muscles. Scott is a very busy man with a lot of responsibility and many people working for him, yet his kindness and personal attention showed me that someone did care. He personally met me for each session and walked me through each machine I was to work on. He never charged me a penny. He always was cheerful, upbeat, and encouraging that things would get better. It was this first glimpse of hope that brought me a modicum of peace, showing me that eventually I would find freedom from pain.

God then handed me over to three of His angels: Joni, Olivia, and Debbie. Each is a specialist: one in physical therapy, another in chiropractic, and the third in kinesiology muscular strengthening. All three have been praying for my condition, and all three are being used to heal my condition. From my teens I insisted I would never go to a chiropractor. Until I met Olivia, I thought all chiropractors were "bone crushers." I never dreamed that I could have a godly one pray for me and be concerned for me as a person.

Knowing the source of my pain has given me new hope. Having friends who are able to work with me is actually a part of the healing process. I now believe my back will be good again someday.

As you'll remember from the introduction, Sandy once said to me, "Wouldn't it be something if God healed you of your pain after you finished this book?" At that time I laughed. Yet a few days ago as I was sitting at the desk, typing away on my laptop computer, I noticed a good portion of the pain is gone.

I'm not sure what all of that means, except that only God can ultimately heal. *How* God heals has always been a mystery to me. I have prayed for some people and seen them instantly healed; others were healed later; and many more were never healed at all. Why? I don't know. I do know that God heals, but I have learned that His methods are never predictable.

Medicine and Healing

My own physical struggle has taught me not to over-spiritualize healing. God can and does use medicine, modern technology, and gifted medical personnel to bring healing to His children. One has only to ride along with the police department in a large city to realize that specially trained paramedics save lives.

I am aware, of course, that some believers say medicine is of the devil. Yet I know that is not true. The capacity of medicine grows as the knowledge of man grows. Researchers discover new cures every day. Measles, polio, tuberculosis, and many lethal diseases that have wiped out millions of people around the world are now under control because of medicine.

Much of medicine finds its roots in plants. There is much to be derived from the plants that the Lord placed here on earth. Scientists have done wonders with plant-based medicines. A recent reports suggests that experts are getting close to the cure for the common cold. In fact, researchers are closing in on cancer, Parkinson's Disease, and other debilitating illnesses.

The question is, Why would God use medicine when He is God? Why not just say the word and cure whoever is ill? I think that question can be answered along with quite a few others of the same nature. God often chooses the quiet over the noisy, the common over the extraordinary, the unceremonious over the showy. Yet He is at work, nonetheless.

I believe it was Alexander the Great who was so impressed with the great wisdom of the famous philosopher Diogenes. Upon meeting Diogenes, Alexander said, "I will do whatever you say to gain your wisdom." Whereupon Diogenes replied, "Okay, then take two dead fish and put them in your pockets for two weeks." Alexander was offended at such a ludicrous suggestion, and he responded, "There's no way I'm going to carry two smelly fish around with me for two weeks." To which the wise Diogenes responded, "What great devotion lost because of two dead fish!"

God can heal however He chooses and with whatever methods seem best to Him. Sometimes He chooses the miraculous; at other times He uses ordinary medicine. But in either case, it is He who heals. We must continually remind ourselves that God is good and that His plans are best for us. We must trust Him and allow Him to heal our hurts however He chooses.

God does heal. When, where, how, and why, we just don't know. So it is easier to try to accept our situation and trust God the Healer to do what He wants done.

Learning the Lessons

My back troubles have taught me several valuable lessons. One is that there is purpose in pain. Pain is a God-installed warning system. If it weren't there, we would severely damage our bodies before we ever knew there was a problem.

As I look back upon my journey through this maze of pain, I can honestly say God had His hand on me all along the way. For so long there was no hope, no hint that the pain would ever leave. Yet God had a plan in it all. By nature I am a very impatient man. God has shown me that it is possible to slow down.

Personal pain also has allowed me to deal with issues I had never brought closure to. Pain has done for me as the psalmist said: "So teach us to number our days, that we may apply our hearts unto wisdom" (Psalm 90:12 KJV). Pain has made me more sensitive to other people who are hurting. Pain has made me grateful that I don't have anything worse. Pain has allowed me to see the tremendous pride that was buried beneath the surface.

I have learned that the Lord will allow pain into our lives to teach us mysteries about ourselves and about Him. Yet He will stop the bleeding and He will dress the hurt. Above all, God is the Healer. Let me emphasize once again that God is in control of our lives for our good. He does not have a plan to use hurt in your life to destroy you.

Remember what Paul wrote in Romans 8:28: "We know that all things work together for good to those who love God, to those who are the called according to His purpose." Let God sit at the control wheel of your life. He'll never steer you wrong. He wants only the best for His children. When at last we learn this wonderful message, we want to pray like the apostle Paul did: "Blessed be the God and Father of our Lord Jesus Christ, who has blessed us with every spiritual blessing in the heavenly places in Christ" (Ephesians 1:3).

Let God's love keep pouring into your life. Let the healings begin, whether they be physical, emotional, spiritual; body, soul, or spirit. Receive the blessings from heaven that are rightfully yours. God knows what will make you happy. He knows you like to have fun. He does too, you know; after all, He is a father.

Our Happy God

Being a father is so awesome—learning about your children and their individual personalities, seeing them smile. Watching them ride their bicycle for the first time. Seeing the wind blowing in their hair. Listening to their first prayers. Being there at graduation. Watching as they pass their driver's test. Walking them down the aisle.

So many things make a father happy. But the happiest a father gets is when his children are happy. Your God is happy to bless you. It makes Him happy to see you happy. And bringing healing to your wounded soul is one of the happiest moments you'll both share. But that healing might come in a package you don't expect.

God's Healing Methods

God can heal us in so many ways. Often God will heal hurts by *teaching*. The Sermon on the Mount is the classic example of this. Through His powerful words, Jesus made healing available to the entire world.

God can also teach us through *experiences*, through the life lessons we learn via hardship, mistakes, or successes.

God's teaching methods are innumerable. He can teach us through a song on the radio or by watching a beautiful sunset or sunrise. I learn a great deal by observation. I love to observe people on the beach, in the airport, shopping, driving, jogging, or just sitting on a curb watching the world go by. Often I drive through the neighborhoods of San Diego and pray for the people I see on the streets, sitting on their porches, or washing their cars. I drive up and down streets I've never visited before, asking the Lord to bless those who live inside the houses I see.

Let God heal you through the teaching found in His Scriptures. Find a good Bible teacher and sit under his instruction. Don't hop from church to church. Settle down and become a part of that church family with your love, giving, and receiving. Get a thorough grasp of the Scriptures, and you will quickly learn that God heals through teaching—mentally, emotionally, physically, and spiritually.

At other times, God heals through direct intervention—through what we might call a miracle. We have seen that God can heal our hurts by working a miracle, as when He restored my mind (although some of my friends question that). We realize that miracles are happening today.

Yet what we call "supernatural" is really only "natural" to the Lord. Miracles are delivered in different-sized packages. The raising of Lazarus from the dead was a "big miracle"; someone finding their lost car keys under a stack of magazines is a "small miracle."

Or perhaps your healing will come not through teaching, not through a miracle, but through modern medicine. If that's the route God chooses for you, then let

Him heal you through modern medicine if He so wills. Let God heal you through prayer if He chooses. But whatever method He chooses, understand that it is He who heals. God is the great Healer.

Begin Your Healing Today

Today is the best day to start trusting God to finish the work that needs to be done in your life. The tender touch of God is ever so near you, my friend. You may be in deep pain physically. You may be in misery mentally. Whatever the problem is, call upon God and trust Him. He is listening and watching you.

The psalmist knew this so well. It is good for us to end with some positive confirmation from the Scriptures. Listen to the Holy Spirit speak to you as you read these words:

> O LORD my God, I cried unto thee, and thou hast healed me (Psalm 30:2 KJV).

The writer affirms that in his trouble he cried to God, and God healed him. We need that encouragement, both you and I. Take it now as it was intended, straight from the loving heart of God. The Lord knows your situation better than you do. Remember the lesson from Job: This isn't about you, this is about God. He is working on a higher and grander plane than any of us can imagine. Though the devil would sift you like wheat, Jesus is interceding on your behalf. So don't give up. God is the Healer. As the psalmist says:

> He sent his word, and healed them, and delivered them from their destructions. Oh that men would praise the LORD for his goodness, and for his wonderful works to the children of men! And let them sacrifice the sacrifices of thanksgiving, and declare his works with rejoicing (Psalm 107:20-22).

O, let us act as the Scripture says. Let us praise the Lord for His goodness to us and for His wonderful works on our behalf. Let us honor Him and let Him know that we recognize Him as the Healer. For that is truly what He is.

My friend, hope in God. Trust in the Lord with all of your heart and lean not to your own understanding. God is the Author and the Finisher of your faith; you are His workmanship. So wait upon the Lord and let the tender touch of God bless you today.

How sweet the name of Jesus sounds
in a believer's ear!
It soothes his sorrows,
heals his wounds,
and drives away his fear.

—John Newton

Notes

CHAPTER ONE—Pain-Distorted Personalities

1. Abe Lemmons quote, *The Bible Illustrator for Windows*, Parsons Technology, 1994.
2. U.S. Bureau of Labor Statistics, 1992.
3. Michael Mantell in *USA Today*, April 5, 1994, p.11A quoting from Mantell and Steve Albrecht, *Ticking Bombs: Defusing Violence in the Workplace* (Burr Ridge, IL: Irwin Professional Books, 1994).
4. Ibid.
5. Ibid.
6. Ibid.
7. Ibid.
8. Ibid.

CHAPTER TWO—Death, the Ultimate Hurt

1. Stuart Hample, et. al., *Children's Letters to God:* The New Collection (New York: Workman Publishing, Co., Inc., 1991).

CHAPTER FOUR—Fallout in the Family

1. *A Judge of the Court of Common Pleas,* U.S. Census Bureau, Toledo, OH, taken from Bible Illustrator, Parsons Technology, Inc, 1990-91. All rights reserved. Used with permission.
2. Ibid.
3. George Barna, *The Frog in the Kettle,* (Ventura, CA: Regal Books, 1990), p. 71.
4. Ann Landers, Syndicated Column, 1988, taken from Bible Illustrator, Parsons Technology, Inc, 1990-91. All rights reserved. Used with permission.
5. James Dobson, "The Marriage Killers," Focus on the Family, Feb. 1993, p. 7.
6. *The State of America's Children Yearbook 1994,* The Children's Defense Fund, Washington, D.C., 1994, pp. 73-99.

CHAPTER FIVE—The Mr. Dillon Syndrome

1. Eric Hoffer, *The Passionate State of Mind* (New York: Harper, 1955), p. 151.

2. "Surfs Up for a Rejuvenated OJ," *People* magazine, June 12, 1978, pp. 44-45.
3. Henry Van Dyke, *The Poems of Henry Van Dyke*, (New York: Charles Scribner & Sons, 1911), p. 260.

CHAPTER SEVEN—Develop a Game Plan

1. Chuck Swindoll, *The Quest for Character* (Portland, OR: Multnomah Press, 1987).

CHAPTER NINE—Tapping into the Power of God

1. George Barna, Barna Research Group

CHAPTER TEN—Clean at Last

1. Larry King, *USA Today*, June 1988, taken from Bible Illustrator, Parsons Technology, Inc, 1990-91. All rights reserved. Used with permission.
2. Taken from Bible Illustrator, Parsons Technology, Inc, 1990-91. All rights reserved. Used with permission.
3. R.G. Lee, taken from Bible Illustrator, Parsons Technology, Inc, 1990-91. All rights reserved. Used with permission.

CHAPTER TWELVE—Basic Equipment

1. Steve Palermo story, *USA Today*, April 5, 1994.

CHAPTER FIFTEEN—Two Are Better Than One

1. Chuck Swindoll, *The Quest for Character* (Portland, OR: Multnomah Press, 1987), pp. 177-81.
2. Henry Penn, taken from Bible Illustrator, Parsons Technology, Inc, 1990-91. All rights reserved. Used with permission.

CHAPTER SIXTEEN—Glimpses of Heaven

1. *The Best of D.L. Moody*, edited by Wilber M. Smith, (Chicago: Moody Press, 1971), pp. 197-99.
2. W. R. Moody & John Ritachie, *The Life of Moody*, (LTD, Kilmarnock, Scotland), p. 474.

Other Good Harvest House Reading

THERE'S HOPE FOR THE HURTING
by *Richard Lee*

Using illustrations from everyday life as well as examples from the lives of Bible personalities, Dr. Lee reminds us that God will restore and redeem those who cry to Him "out of the depths."

YOU'RE NEVER ALONE
by *Marie Shropshire*

In *You're Never Alone,* you will discover that God is your ever-present helper. By accepting His friendship, God is a friend who never leaves us alone. He will release you from your bondage of fear, anxiety and loneliness.

WHY GRACE CHANGES EVERYTHING
by *Chuck Smith*

In this deeply relational book, Pastor Chuck Smith shares from Scripture and from his heart on 12 great themes of grace. He shows how grace transforms duty, guilt, and failure into enthusiastic service, laughter, and a life worth living.

EVERY DAY WITH JESUS
by *Greg Laurie*

Make each day an adventure of spiritual discovery and growth. These brief, powerful meditations, rooted in God's Word and sprinkled with good humor, invite you to take an intimate walk with the Savior.